An Outline History of the
Railways of Nottinghamshire

Michael A. Vanns

Nottinghamshire
County Council

Acknowledgements

For taking the trouble to record the railways in the county over many years, the author would like to thank all the photographers whose pictures have been used in this book. The presentation of railway histories would be the poorer without them. Acknowledgement also goes to the custodians of the negatives and prints who are still prepared to make images available for works such as this. For giving the author the opportunity to write this brief history and then supporting his efforts thanks must go to Mark Dorrington, Assistant Head, Archives, Heritage and Records Management at Nottinghamshire Archives and Tim Warner of the Nottinghamshire Libraries and Archives Publications Group.

ISBN: 978-0-902751-67-5

Printed and designed by: Nottinghamshire County Council, Design and Print, 2010-08-25

Contents

Please Note : The sketch maps included within the text of this book are intended as quick reference guides only. They show regularly used passenger lines but do not include those which were used solely for goods or freight.

Introduction

Perhaps the two most obvious questions that may be asked of the railways in Nottinghamshire are, why does the country's premier electrified main line pass through Newark and Retford and not the city of Nottingham? Why do the fastest trains between London and Yorkshire race through either Newark or on a line up the Erewash Valley midway between Nottingham and Derby? These questions are even more relevant when you discover that Nottingham was once on two through south to north main lines, one passing right through a spacious station in the heart of the city. Surprisingly, just four words can be used in answer, which together neatly encapsulate Nottinghamshire's railway history; coal, geography, competition, and politics.

Before the first railways as we would recognise them today were built in the county, Nottinghamshire had thirteen working coalmines. By 1862 that figure had risen to 21, those pits producing 733,000 tons of coal annually. In the years before the First World War (1914-18) there were 42 collieries at work and just over 12 million tons of coal was extracted, the majority of it loaded into 10 or 12 ton, wooden-sided railway wagons for transport around the country to feed the boilers of thousands of steam engines that drove the machinery of iron-works, breweries, steel mills, timber yards, cotton mills, as well as powering the boilers of ocean liners, battleships, fishing trawlers and heating the homes of millions of people. By 1930 production had risen to 14.5 million tons a year, (compared with a decline over the border in Derbyshire), followed after World War II by the creation of Nottinghamshire's so-called 'super pits' at Calverton (1952), Cotgrave (1964), and Bevercotes (1965) - each intended to raise 1m tons a year.

It was coal and geography that put Nottingham on a branch line at the very end of the 1830s (see Chapter One); twenty years later it was competition with the company which ran that branch line – the Midland Railway company (MR) - that spurred on the Great Northern Railway (GNR) to route its main line through Newark and Retford (see Chapter Two). From that time onwards, and for the next one hundred years, coal and passenger traffic dominated railway politics in the county. In the 1870s and 1880s the GNR pushed new lines into the Nottinghamshire coalfields in direct competition with the MR. In the same period the MR put Nottingham on a new through route between London, Yorkshire and Scotland. Twenty years later at the very end of the 19th century, competition with both the MR and GNR for Yorkshire passenger traffic to and from the capital led the Manchester, Sheffield & Lincolnshire Railway (MS&LR, later renamed the Great Central Railway - GCR) to place Nottingham at the centre of its brand new main line with a palatial central station – Nottingham Victoria (see Chapter Three).

A little over 60 years later national politics destroyed both those cross-city routes in the interests of economy and returned Nottingham (in railway terms) to its pre-1880 status. In the same period, the railways were still vital in moving coal from the new Nottinghamshire 'super pits' to the second generation of electricity generating power stations located along the banks of the Trent at High Marnham (1959), Staythorpe 'B' (1962), West Burton (1967), Cottam (1968) and Ratcliffe-on-Soar (at full capacity, 1969). Barely twenty years later, through the late 1980s and into the 1990s, however, all that had changed with the number of Nottinghamshire pits reduced to a rump of just five and the British economy dependent on imported coal and oil. Then in 1984, central government financed British Rail to electrify the former GNR main line between London and Yorkshire and onwards to Edinburgh, thus providing Newark by 1991 with a faster and more frequent service to the capital than anything then available from the city of Nottingham (see Chapter Six). At the time of writing (2010) that disparity still continues, with the fastest train between London and Newark (193km/120 miles) taking only 1hr 16min, and the fastest London-Nottingham service (204.3km/127 miles) taking 1hr 44min. Of coal traffic still to be observed on Nottinghamshire's railways, the majority is imported: Thoresby Colliery in Sherwood Forest is the only local colliery still in operation.

Excluding colliery lines (over which there were never any regular passenger services), the railway map of Nottinghamshire was created in just 78 years between 1839 and 1917 by the three private companies mentioned above with the addition of the Lancashire, Derbyshire & East Coast Railway (LD&ECR) that enjoyed a brief independent existence (1896-1907) before being absorbed into the GCR (see Chapter Four). The MR, GNR and GCR dominated the county's railway services until the first rationalisation of Britain's railways in 1923 (see Chapter Five). Other companies did make inroads into the county before that date but they were always minor players.

When considering how Nottinghamshire's railways developed, and why the routes that we are familiar with today were chosen, it is vital to remember that all 19th century railway companies were formed with the primary purpose of making money for their shareholders. Although their plans were subject to Parliamentary scrutiny and needed an Act of Parliament in order to raise the necessary funds for construction, they were built to generate income for their investors. There was no strategic national railway plan and lines were built simply because a group of individuals believed there was money to be made. The necessary support was won and the opposition bought off by promising all manner of benefits that would result from railway connection; cheaper coal for industry and domestic use; increased market opportunities for traders and manufacturers; access to better vegetables for the local population. But these promises were only a means to an end, and if a railway could be built serving the same area as an already established line by promising better returns and lower rates, then duplication of infrastructure and services was not an issue. The result of this sort of private enterprise in Nottinghamshire was a concentration of lines in the west of the county, in the coalfields of the Erewash, and Leen Valleys and (by the end of the century) to the west and north of Mansfield. The greatest financial rewards came from transporting minerals out of these areas. The population of Sutton-in-Ashfield never warranted four railway stations and three competing passengers services to and from Nottingham. The fact the community ended up with four stations (see Chapter Four) was simply a by-product of competition between three railway companies, each set on making money from coal.

The heyday for making money by transporting goods and people by rail was the period between 1890 and the start of the First World War in 1914. Nottinghamshire, as with every other area in the British Isles, could rightly call these the halcyon days of railway communication. After that, although the physical railway map remained largely unchanged, shareholders, managers, and directors never achieved the financial returns they had before the War. The government, having run the railways itself during the conflict, forced a rationalisation plan on the country's private railway companies in 1923: the MR was absorbed into the London, Midland & Scottish Railway (LMS), whilst the GNR and GCR were brought together as the London & North Eastern Railway (LNER) group. Tiny concessions were made to reduce operating costs between 1923 and the outbreak of the Second World War, but the Victorian infrastructure remained stubbornly intact with trains of old carriages being pulled by ageing steam locomotives over lines which were increasingly losing their passengers to motor buses.

After the War it was only the pride of running an independent company that set the directors of the LMS and the LNER against nationalisation. But the truth was that there was no more money to be made. In the euphoria of a socialist landslide in the first post-war General Election the railways were nationalised in 1948. Modernisation was promised and expected, and in the coal and electricity generating industries – both newly nationalised as well - that proved to be the case. But on the railways there were few immediate signs of change. Passenger services did not improve and buses followed by the private motor car soon proved to be a better alternative than travelling by train. In the 1950s and 60s Nottinghamshire enthusiastically embraced road improvements in line with almost every British county. It was left to Dr Beeching to try and make the country's railways pay and within the space of just six years between the publication of his report 'The Reshaping of British Railways' in 1963 and the withdrawal of the last Nottingham to London Marylebone service in 1969, the county's rail network was cut back to such an extent that it resembled a railway map of the 1850s. And for people in Mansfield wishing to travel by train, it took them back to a time even before railways!

In many ways, the paralysing shock of Beeching's extensive rationalisation lasted well into the 1980s, further reinforced after the failed miners' strike of 1985, by the closure of almost all the county's collieries and, consequently, the loss of all locally generated rail-borne coal traffic. Modernisation, once such an optimistic word, became synonymous with cutbacks, closures and thousands of job losses. That such savage cuts had been made in two state-owned industries – British Rail and British Coal, both born of socialist ideals following the Second World War, and theoretically run for the benefit of the community - was particularly hard for many people to accept. Only after the death of post-war socialism and the neutering of union power that occurred in the 1980s did some confidence in railways as a viable means of transport return. Road congestion and a growing unease with new road building and

pollution further helped this reassessment. New funding became available and local authorities were given more opportunities to become involved in local transport. Then came the Conservative government's Railway Privatisation Act of 1993 (effective from 1st April 1994) and the belief that railways could once again make money for private companies and their shareholders. Many observers (including railway historians) believed that this was really an illusion, but it certainly gave the railways a new lease of life.

Considering that the railways of Nottinghamshire were originally built and operated by just a handful of private companies, it is one of those historical absurdities that in the decade following privatisation, more organisations have been involved in running or leasing services and in maintaining trains and track than at any time in their history. The only significant differences between the two periods, of course, is that none of these present-day companies has built one mile of new track, whilst all have received substantial, but indirect, government financial subsidies for running their businesses.

The last expansion of the network in Nottinghamshire - if it can be so called - was the reinstatement of the line between Nottingham and Mansfield (and onwards to Worksop) achieved in the years between 1993 and 1998. Although completed after privatisation, the plans and determination to succeed in this venture sprang from a collaboration between local government and a nationalised industry - British Rail.

The following chapters aim to make some sense of the complex story of railways in Nottinghamshire between 1839 and 2010. This is not a definitive history. Much information has, by necessity, been omitted and, equally, one author is never able to know everything there is to know about his subject. For those seeking more detail, a select bibliography is included.

The Great Northern Railway's signalbox at Codnor Park station, built in 1875. The design was only used for a handful of structures and all of those were in Nottinghamshire. It is an excellent example of the quality of Victorian craftsmanship and their attention to details such as the 45degree boarding and the brackets supporting the geometric barge board. When this photograph was taken in the first decade of the twentieth century, the signalbox would have been painted in three tones of brown, with the name board of white letters on a black background, given a red border. Notice also the little box of flowers next to the landing.

The GNR's Codnor Park station - opened to passengers on 1st August 1876 - was on the Nottinghamshire side of the River Erewash barely half a mile from the Midland Railway's station – opened on 6th September 1847 - that was in Derbyshire. Renamed Jacksdale in July 1950, the GNR station closed on 7th January 1963, followed four years later by the MR's station. *(author's collection)*

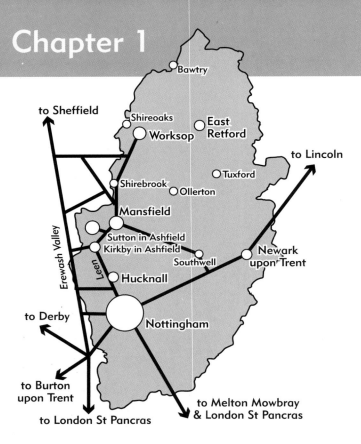

Chapter 1

The Midland Railway

The majority of trains serving Nottinghamshire today run over lines built between 1839 and 1875 by the former Midland Railway (MR) and its predecessor the Midland Counties Railway (MCR). Today, passengers account for almost all the income generated on this rail network but, for over a hundred years, coal was the biggest earner, and the MR prospered from, and was shaped by, its transportation.

The Erewash Valley separating Nottinghamshire from Derbyshire had a long history of coalmining, and by 1797 canals ran down the valley from Pinxton to the River Trent, into Nottingham and onwards to Grantham. The River Trent provided connections eastwards through Newark to the Humber Estuary, west via the Trent & Mersey Canal through the Potteries to the Mersey and Liverpool, and southwards by the Grand Union Canal to London via Leicester (completed in 1805). The canal network was soon earning its investors good dividends, but within a few years entrepreneurs elsewhere in Derbyshire, Shropshire, South Wales and - more significantly - in the North-East were demonstrating the benefits of using wagons with iron wheels running on iron rails. The first* such arrangement in Nottinghamshire was a horse-drawn railway

opened in 1819 from Pinxton Wharf, on a branch of the Cromford Canal, to Mansfield. The line was, in effect, an extension to the canal carrying coal from Erewash pits into Mansfield and stone in the opposite direction.

There were no further significant railway developments in the East Midlands until a new line between the coalfields around Swannington and Leicester was opened in 1832. This new line allowed the price of Leicestershire coal to drop below that of coal brought via canal from the Erewash Valley. Mine owners in Nottinghamshire and Derbyshire immediately retaliated against their Leicestershire neighbours by planning to build their own railway down the Erewash Valley to Leicester. Lancashire investors were persuaded to help finance plans for this Midland Counties Railway (MCR) and they brought with them even more ambitious ideas. In their region the opening of the Liverpool & Manchester Railway in 1830 had demonstrated the unexpected popularity of people travelling by train, and in 1835 they persuaded the MCR to push its line on from Leicester to Rugby where it could join the planned London & Birmingham Railway. This would give access to the capital for both coal and passengers and, by two easy branches, connect Derby (via the Derwent Valley) and Nottingham (via the Trent Valley) to the main north-south route.

With the benefit of hindsight, the way these additions were grafted onto the existing plans adversely affected all Nottingham's future railway development. At Derby the MCR was to link with two other new lines – the North Midland Railway (NMR) and the Birmingham & Derby Junction Railway (BDJR), which would immediately make that county town an important railway junction on a strategic through route. Nottingham, by contrast, was to be simply the end of a branch. This disadvantage was appreciated, and complained about, at the time, but no other company had a viable alternative. As a result, at the very end of May 1839, in fields to the south of Nottingham, and separated from the town by the Nottingham Canal, a modest terminal station was opened for passengers (1). At first trains ran only between Nottingham and Derby, but from July 1840, when

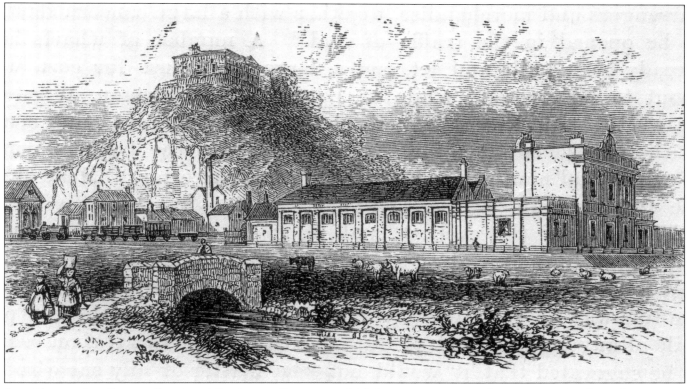

1. Long before Queens Road and Carrington Street were laid down, an artist stood approximately where the two roads would join, looking back at Nottingham Castle to sketch this view of the original MCR station.
    (engraving from 'Midland Railway', F.S. Williams, 5th edition 1886)

2. The MCR's bridge over the River Trent, (the iron spans cast by the Butterley Co, Derbyshire), taking the railway southwards through Redhill Tunnel, seen on the right, to Leicester and Rugby.
    (engraving from 'Midland Railway', F.S. Williams, 5th edition 1886)

3.   An early 20th century photograph of the Nottingham-Lincoln line crossing Colwick Road, Nottingham. On the right, covered in creepers, is the 1840s crossing keepers house, whilst opposite is the later 1893 signalbox. *(author's collection)*

4.   This photograph of Southwell station looking towards Mansfield was probably taken shortly after the First World War. Prominent on the left are the lime-washed cattle pens. *(author's collection)*

the extension to Rugby (via Leicester) was fully opened, passengers from both county towns had their very first opportunity to travel to and from London (Euston) by train. The Rugby line branched off the existing MCR route approximately halfway between Nottingham and Derby just south of Long Eaton, and because the rivers Trent and Erewash define the south-western boundary of Nottinghamshire in this area, the junction was actually in Derbyshire. As the Rugby line headed south, however, it crossed the Trent (2) which brought it back into Nottinghamshire, passing through Redhill Tunnels, through the wayside station at Kegworth, before entering Leicestershire just north of Loughborough.

During its independent existence, the MCR never managed to build its 'main' Erewash Valley line. That was left to the Midland Railway (MR), an 1844 amalgamation of the MCR, the NMR and the BDJR, who built a line between Trent Junction and Codnor Park ironworks which opened in the summer of 1847. (Almost all of this route lies in Derbyshire and, therefore, strictly speaking is outside the scope of this book. However, coalmining and iron and steel making along the whole of the Erewash Valley, shaped and influenced railway developments in the west of Nottinghamshire throughout the 19th century.)

By the time the Erewash Valley line opened, the MR had managed to put Nottingham on a through route by extending eastwards (3), to Newark and Lincoln (1846) but only because it wanted to reach those two places ahead of the Great Northern Railway (GNR) whose plans it had managed to delay but not completely defeat in Parliament during the Railway Mania of 1845. In that year, hundreds of speculative railways were promoted in every part of the British Isles, including a number that could have placed Nottingham on through routes running north-south and east-west. Supporters of two independent railways between Derbyshire and Boston via Newark, and from

Nottingham to Mansfield were successfully bought off by the MR during this period, the company opening its own line in October 1848 up the Leen Valley to Kirkby-in-Ashfield on the Mansfield & Pinxton Railway, which it had acquired that year. Almost exactly a year later it upgraded the latter so that trains could run into Mansfield. In contrast, assurances made to investors in the more ambitious east to west railway – the Boston, Newark & Sheffield Railway - were only partly honoured. As part of what would have been the central section of that cross-country route, the MR opened a branch from its Nottingham-Lincoln line between (what later became) Rolleston Junction and Southwell with promises to extend it when funds allowed. The branch opened in July 1847 only to close two years later. It reopened in April 1852 only to close once again the following March. Trains began to run again in September 1860 and this time they continued. In 1871 the branch was pushed further westwards as single track to join with the Nottingham & Mansfield line (4). By then, however, the promises given to the 1845 investors in the rival scheme had been quietly forgotten.

Like any other business, the MR's primary focus was the making not the spending of money and a line between Southwell and Mansfield was unremunerative. Better rewards were to be had elsewhere in Nottinghamshire or, more accurately, in the coalfields. The Erewash Valley line had been pushed a little further northwards from Codnor Park to Pye Bridge in 1850, and in the following year a new connection was laid from Pye Bridge to Pinxton to link up with the Leen Valley line. Of more significance, the Erewash Valley line was extended northwards ten years later breaking through its watershed (via Alfreton Tunnel) to join the former NMR's Derby-Rotherham line at Clay Cross. This extension opened for goods in November 1861 and for passenger trains in May the following year. Within twenty years this route was being used by the MR's principal Anglo-

Scottish passenger trains, as well as endless goods and mineral trains nose to tail delivering raw materials to the blast furnaces and ironworks at Clay Cross and Stanton (just over the border in Derbyshire), and Bennerley, and Codnor Park. By 1902 extra lines for these slow moving trains had been added almost all the way south from Chesterfield to London, and just within the Nottinghamshire border, Toton Sidings had grown from modest beginnings in the 1850s to become one of the country's largest marshalling yards, working twenty-four hours a day, seven days a week (5). In 1901 the Toton marshalling yard had been remodelled so that wagons could be 'hump shunted' the aim being to speed up the sorting of wagons into trains.

A similar investment occurred in the Leen Valley during the same period. In 1875 the existing line was extended from Mansfield to a junction between Shireoaks and Worksop on the Manchester, Sheffield & Lincolnshire Railway (MS&LR). Before the route was complete, a new and impressive station was opened at Mansfield in 1872. From there, the extension pushed northwards, striding across the town on a 15 arch curving stone viaduct (6). Once opened in 1875, the MR gained running powers over the MS&LR's line to Retford and, more importantly, into Shireoaks Colliery the first of Nottinghamshire's deep coal mines in the 'concealed' coalfield that had been winning coal since 1859. By coincidence, this was the same year in which the MS&LR's Retford passenger station had closed with all services being concentrated on the GNR's station. Inevitably, this company was not prepared to see its rival, the MR, run Mansfield services into its Retford station, so the MS&LR was obliged to use its engines for all trains between Worksop and Retford.

By the beginning of 20th century the MR had connections to ten collieries along the Leen Valley line within Nottinghamshire and nine in the

Erewash valley south of Alfreton (in both Derbyshire and Nottinghamshire). The MR's monopoly in both coalfields, however, had not survived unchallenged for in 1875 the GNR had opened its own route into the Erewash, followed by an extension three years later into the heart of the MR's empire – Derby. By the autumn of 1881 an even more lucrative incursion had been made up the Leen Valley with a further extension northwards achieved by 1901 (see Chapter Two). The MR had retaliated by strengthening its cross-valley connections firstly with a line between Bennerley Junction (Erewash Valley) and Basford Junction (Leen Valley), and then another between Radford Junction (Leen Valley) and Trowell Junction (Erewash Valley). The first mentioned was in reality two colliery branches joined together and as a through route it had a very short life, some of the tracks west of Kimberley being lifted during the First World War never to be reinstated.

More important was the MR's second connecting line between Radford and Trowell Junction. Opened in 1875, it too served a colliery, the long-established Wollaton pit, and although the line was insignificant in itself for local passengers, it soon became part of a much larger improvement scheme for Nottingham's travelling public which by stitching together existing routes and building two new ones outside the county, finally put the county town on a through north-south route from London. Until then, journeys to and from the capital for Nottingham passengers had been slow and inconvenient. Before 1858 all MR trains had been run in and out of the London & North Western Railway's (LNWR) terminus at Euston and a typical journey took between three and a half and seven hours. From February that year, when the MR's new Leicester-Hitchin line was opened, all trains were diverted into the GNR's Kings Cross station but a trip to London remained a challenge. The majority of Nottingham passengers were still obliged to travel via Derby or brave using a small platform to change trains where the lines from

5.   The majority of loaded coal wagons seen in this first decade of the 20th century view of the eastern (up) side of Toton yard belonged to the MR, graphically illustrating just how much fuel was needed to keep a fleet of steam locomotives running. The down yard 'hump' can just been seen in the background. *(author's collection)*

6.   Church Street, Mansfield, photographed just before the First World War, showing the carriages of a local MR train on the viaduct. *(Valentines Series postcard, author's collection)*

13

7. This handsome 4-4-0 locomotive designed by S.W. Johnson and built with others of its class between 1900 and 1901 at Derby, would have been brand new when photographed approaching Widmerpool station bound for Nottingham. *(photo: Rev. T.B. Parley)*

8. Nottingham's crowded MR goods yard photographed on 27th March 1922. The seven storey grain warehouse was opened in 1851 with the adjacent warehouse with four pitched roofs completed in 1896 on the site of the MCR's 1839 station. All were demolished and eventually replaced by the city's magistrates court. *(National Railway Museum: detail from official MR photograph DY12458)*

Derby, Nottingham and Leicester (and Rugby) met. This junction was provided with a proper station – christened Trent – in 1862, and from October 1868 at least the London destination had improved with all passenger trains running to and from the MR's own impressive terminus at St Pancras. Even so journey times for Nottingham passengers did not improve significantly until the summer of 1880 when London-Bradford & Leeds expresses were re-routed via Nottingham. Approaching from the south on a new line from Melton Mowbray (7) that entered the county between the stations of Old Dalby and Upper Broughton, the expresses continued their journey into Yorkshire over the Radford-Trowell line without having to reverse in Nottingham station. Overnight, Nottingham and London were less than three hours apart and, after February 1882, served by through Anglo-Scottish trains. At last the MR had a London service for Nottinghamshire travellers to rival that offered by the GNR in the east of the county.

From the 1880s until the beginning of the First World War, services offered by the MR and the infrastructure of Nottinghamshire's railways improved enormously. By the close of the 19th century the facilities for goods traffic had been completely overhauled with many substantial new buildings erected; the ones that survived until the 1990s on what is now the site of the magistrates court in Nottingham, for example, were particularly impressive (8). Hucknall station was completely rebuilt in 1895 to serve a population that had increased five-fold since the line first opened, but the last flourish of the MR's independent existence was completed in 1904 when the final section of the new Nottingham passenger station fronting Carrington Street was opened (9). It replaced the 1848 station that had in its turn superseded the original MCR terminus of 1839.

In the decade prior to the outbreak of the First World War, the MR had become, like all the country's railway companies, a complex operation its staff governed by hundreds of pages of rules and regulations and special notices, with forms to cover every situation that could possibly arise on a busy railway. It is almost impossible to give the 21st century reader any meaningful impression of the complexity of running the MR's business a hundred years ago when there were thousands of passengers and goods services available. The public passenger timetable for the summer of 1903, for example, ran to 184 pages, printed in small, closely packed type with no fewer than 48 additional pages covering excursions. Information was given for everything from the price of tickets to the rates for transporting sheep. Passengers could book special tickets to every part of the British Isles, and beyond. For example, a First Class return ticket to the Isle of Man cost 37/4 (£1.86), luncheon baskets were available for those travelling by overnight sleeper trains and connections were made to all the major sea ports. A First Class return between Nottingham and Cork, via Bristol (including a cabin on the boat) cost 34/9 (£1.73) for example, whilst a Third Class one month return to Paris via Dover, was priced at 90/4 (£4.51). By 1903 holidays were part of almost everyone's experience, but for the truly hardy Edwardian the MR offered some amazing walking and cycling tours. Originating from Nottingham there were 30 different tours available, and the following is just one example of what was on offer. Tour No.27 offered the severest endurance test of all by taking the third class cyclist and his or her machine by train to Doncaster, from where peddle-power was required to propel the explorer 72 miles down the Great North Road through Newark to Stamford from where a train could be caught back to Nottingham, all for a mere 5/4 (26p), plus 2/- (10p) for the bicycle or 3/- (15p) for a tandem.

On 1 January 1923 the MR was merged into the London, Midland & Scottish Railway (LMS). By then the railway was a completely different machine to what it had been in 1845. In 1845 it

9. Nottingham's impressive MR station of 1904. In the middle distance the GCR strides across the site. The MR's 1848 station buildings were situated on Station Road between the two footbridges linking the platforms. In the middle of the background is the GNR's London Road, Low Level station and immediately to the left of the gas holder, London Road, High Level station. In the left foreground is the MR's goods depot. *(Nottingham Central Library: Local Studies Collection 2116)*

10. Two very young Edwardian trainspotters slightly in awe of the MR 0-4-0T steam engine in 'crimson lake' livery and its crew at Nottingham station. *(Nottingham Central Library: Local Studies Collection/ Nottingham Historical Film Unit)*

was a new ambitious, but still provincial company - an uneasy amalgamation of three railways radiating from Derby, all entirely dependent on other companies for access to London, the major British ports, Wales and Scotland. At the end of its independent existence the MR was one of the most profitable railway companies in the country had the grandest London terminus of any company (St Pancras), could boast direct services to both the west and east coasts, and had what we would describe today as a distinctive brand image; standardisation had stamped its mark on everything from locomotives (10) to signalboxes (11), stations to staff uniform (12). That legacy lasted a long time.

* Whilst the Mansfield-Pinxton Railway may be identified as the county's first to run on iron rails, historical documents show that Nottinghamshire can boast of having one of the very first railways of any kind anywhere in the country when as early as 1604 a line of timber rails was laid from coal pits around Wollaton to Nottingham. Unfortunately this route of 1604 spawned no imitators and it was to be in the Erewash Valley where the county's railway history really began over two hundred years later.

11. The interior of the MR's Lenton South Signalbox photographed a few years before the First World War. Both the timber signalbox and the frame of levers were made at Derby to standard designs replicated all over the company's routes. *(author's collection)*

12. By the time this photograph of Pinxton & Selston station was taken just before the First World War, the Mansfield & Pinxton line of 1819 had been upgraded by the MR and transformed by the installation of its standard equipment. The brick buildings dated to the reopening of the station at the end of 1851; the signals were made with hundreds of identical ones at Derby; the signalbox was an example of the latest standard MR design when it opened in 1897; and the staff look smart in their corporate uniforms. *(Lens of Sutton)*

Chapter 2

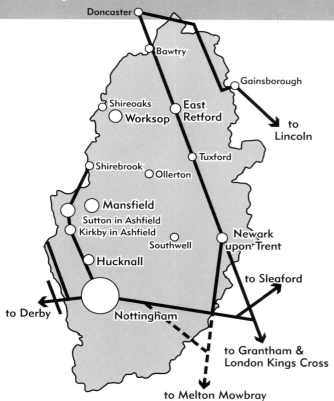

The Great Northern Railway

Unlike the MR, born in the coalfields of Nottinghamshire and Derbyshire, the initial intention of the Great Northern Railway (GNR) was to pass through Nottinghamshire as quickly as possible. The county just happened to be on the route of its planned grand new line between London and York.

The GNR was a child of the rivalry between a number of speculators whose schemes had started to appear in the 1830s. These plans became more focused and practical after 1840 when the very first steam-hauled trains started to run between London and York (from Euston to Rugby over the London & Birmingham Railway, onwards over the Midland Counties Railway (MCR) to Derby, northwards on the North Midland Railway to Normanton (east of Wakefield), and then on to York via the York & North Midland Railway). By 1844 there were firm proposals up before Parliamentary scrutiny for rival routes and it was by no means certain that Nottinghamshire would

benefit from the passage of a London-York railway at all. Three of the contenders favoured routes via Lincoln to take their lines through the East Midlands with only one company – the GNR – looking to push its main line through Grantham, Newark and Doncaster to the Yorkshire capital. After amalgamating with a rival and flirting with the idea of passing midway between Newark and Lincoln with branches to both places, the GNR's plans prevailed, eventually receiving Parliamentary approval in June 1846. For such a huge undertaking (the largest single railway development until then) it was inevitable that the work took some years to complete with a number of changes of plan during construction. Retford and Doncaster were connected by the summer of 1849 but the central section of the main line between Retford and Peterborough was not completed for another three years. York was destined never to be reached by GNR tracks - the company's trains had to use those of other companies beyond Doncaster. The GNR entered Nottinghamshire from Lincolnshire between Claypole and Balderton, disdainfully crossed the MR's Nottingham-Lincoln line at 45 degrees on the level at Newark, and then exited the north of the county for Yorkshire at Bawtry.

As soon as the main line was completed in 1852 the benefits for Nottinghamshire travellers were immediate. Overnight for those living in Retford a journey to or from London by the fastest train was now possible in three and three quarter hours. To and from Newark the times were a little over three and a quarter hours. Even from the village station at Carlton-on-Trent (13) London could be reached in just over 4½ hours, whilst even passengers from Nottingham living 23 miles (37km) away could benefit from GNR trains. Only a day after the GNR started to run passenger trains over the newly completed main line between Peterborough and Retford, it was offering Nottingham people the opportunity to travel on its trains from the MR's station to London via Grantham. The best service took about four hours, the same time as the fastest MR train to London Euston, but considerably better

13.　The GNR main line at Carlton-on-Trent photographed in the first decade of the 20th century. The station buildings seen in the background did not alter between their construction in 1851/2 and their demolition a little over one hundred years later. The crossing keepers cottage of the same date lasted a little longer and the signalbox, seen here in its original 1875 state, was pulled down in 1977. *(author's collection)*

14.　The reason for the huge Great Northern Railway board on the Ambergate, Nottingham & Boston & Eastern Junction Railway's Nottingham, London Road station, was to ensure it could be seen from the rival MR station. At the time this photograph was taken – c.1898 - GNR trains were yet to be diverted into Victoria station. *(photo: S.W.A. Newton/the Record Office for Leicestershire, Leicester & Rutland:X6/4)*

than most other MR trains (the slowest of which could take fully nine and a half hours to complete its journey).

The GNR service had been made possible by a junction at Grantham with the Ambergate, Nottingham & Boston & Eastern Junction Railway who had an agreement with the MR to run trains into that company's Nottingham station. So incensed was the MR with what it considered an abuse of this agreement that only minutes after the engine of the first GNR train to arrive in Nottingham had been detached from its carriages in Nottingham station it was hemmed in by MR locomotives and manoeuvred off to a shed where the track was removed so as to imprison it. It took seven months of legal wrangling before the engine was released during which time conciliatory GNR suggestions of an amalgamation between the two companies were dismissed by the MR.

From April 1853 the GNR consolidated its position in Nottingham by leasing and operating the 'Ambergate', and supporting its decision to build an independent station into which, naturally, GNR trains from Grantham and London, Kings Cross could run. That station, just off London Road, opened in October 1857 (14) and with a touch of irony, typical of railway politics at this period, only four months later, all MR passenger trains between Nottingham and London were also being run in and out of the GNR's terminus at Kings Cross via the MR's new line between Leicester and Hitchin. This arrangement continued until St Pancras - the MR's own station in the capital – was opened in October 1868.

The Ambergate, Nottingham & Boston & Eastern Junction Railway had been one of hundreds of similar mid-1840s companies born of the so-called 'Railway Mania'. Its aspirations were initially as large as those of the GNR but, unlike the latter, it failed to achieve its goals. In some railway books the 'Ambergate' is dismissed as a minor player with a silly name, but that is an unfair assessment. The

company name was typical of many of its period and simply described its route. Its aim was to connect at Ambergate with other railways planning lines south-eastwards out of Manchester. From Ambergate it got Parliamentary approval for its own line via Nottingham to the docks at Boston on the east coast, already shipping coal transported by river and canal from the Nottinghamshire & Derbyshire coalfield. Providing a new outlet for Nottinghamshire coal and the products of Lancashire mills, as well as opening up new markets for Baltic timber in the north-west, was a sound business plan and, if successful, would have proved the making of the Ambergate. In the end it could only raise sufficient funds to complete a line between Nottingham and Grantham and what could have been a truly grand railway never fully materialised.

What the Ambergate did achieve for the GNR, however, was ultimately of more significance than a route for Nottingham-London passenger services. It gave the GNR a base from where it could tap into the lucrative Nottinghamshire and Derbyshire coalfields. In 1863, by agreeing not to proceed with a line of its own into the Erewash Valley, the GNR had secured advantageous rates for a share of the coal coming over MR lines into exchange sidings at the Ambergate's Nottingham station (from where it continued its journey southwards via Grantham to London). This 'Coal Traffic Agreement' remained uneasily in force until 1871 when, due to many changed circumstances, the MR altered its terms, immediately prompting the GNR to revive its independent railway scheme.

In 1873, after fierce opposition from the MR, the GNR secured Parliamentary approval for its own railway into the Erewash Valley, and for a new route between Nottingham, Derby and Stafford. The most lucrative section for the GNR was that between Pinxton and a new marshalling yard at Netherfield (christened Colwick Yard) on the Nottingham-Grantham line. Connections were made to the collieries at Pinxton, Langton (1844),

Riddings(?), Plumptre (1850), High Park (1854), Selston & Moor Green (1874), and Digby (1866). Thus whilst there were nine passenger stations on the new line it was certainly not built for their convenience, but for the most effective transportation of coal. Coal trains started to use the new route between Pinxton and Colwick yard (15) from August 1875. The branch to Derby opened to passengers in 1878, and GNR trains finally reached Stafford in 1881 by running over existing lines belonging to the North Staffordshire Railway and by the purchase of the unremunerative Stafford & Uttoxeter Railway.

In the same year that the GNR reached Stafford, the company launched itself more profitably northwards up the Leen Valley from just north of Basford to Annesley reaching the more modern and deeper Nottinghamshire pits. A decade later this route was pushed still further northwards, once again as a result of inter-company rivalry and the quest for coal. The MS&LR, having pushed its new and impressive main line southwards through Nottingham and on to London, had upset the GNR. Some compensation was to be had from a number of concessions extracted from the MS&LR one of which was the right to run GNR trains through the new Annesley Tunnel under Robin Hood's Hills. Spared the expense of boring its own tunnel, the GNR was then able to extend its Leen Valley line from a junction with the MS&LR just north of the tunnel to Shirebrook. In very difficult stages between 1897 and 1900, the line was extended steadily towards its Derbyshire destination. To reach Summit Pit (opened 1887) a deep, long cutting had to be excavated east of Kirkby-in-Ashfield and the route through Sutton-in-Ashfield was no less difficult in order to be able to drive a short branch west to the collieries of Silverhill (opened 1875) and Teversal (opened

15. A proud group of early twentieth century GNR employees belonging to the 1877 Colwick Junction Branch of the National Union of Railwaymen of England, Ireland and Scotland and Wales. As well as the title, the banner proclaims 'we assist the widows and fatherless'. *(author's collection)*

16.   A long, London-bound, coal train from Colwick yard approaching Radcliffe-on-Trent station, c.1922, pulled by a type of locomotive nicknamed for obvious reasons a 'Long Tom'. At the time there were 24 similar engines out of a total of 167 shedded at Colwick. *(photo: H.L. Salmon)*

1869). The line then wound its way to link up with the collieries of Pleasley (sunk 1872, opened 1878) and Shirebrook (opened 1896 / 7), just over the border in Derbyshire, before finally reaching the Lancashire, Derbyshire & East Coast Railway (LD&ECR) at Langwith Junction (see Chapter Four). As a result of this expansion, the rapidly growing community at Skegby gained a passenger station, as did Sutton-in-Ashfield, Teversal and Pleasley, all three already served by the MR. Despite its population having more than doubled between 1881 and 1901 from around 4,000 to just over 10,000 people, Kirkby-in-Ashfield was not provided with a GNR station. That, however, was no hardship as the community was already served by three stations within a one mile radius of the old town centre. Nearby Mansfield had witnessed a similar rapid growth in population (from just over 13,500 to nearly 21,500) but the GNR remained

unmoved following three requests from the Town Council for a connecting line.

With new collieries now connected to the GNR the amount of coal reaching Colwick yard was greatly increased. By 1901 Colwick was not just handling coal traffic but had also become the GNR's centre in the East Midlands for the reception and distribution of iron ore, timber, stone, milk, beer, fruit, vegetable, fish and other perishable goods. In 1899 the GNR finished its huge new £1m goods station in Deansgate, Manchester beginning a tradition of night-time express goods trains between there and London Kings Cross, running via Colwick yard. Colwick also handled the nocturnal beer trains which regularly plied between Burton-on-Trent and Newcastle via Newark as well as the milk trains from the Derbyshire & Staffordshire Extension line, hundreds of gallons sent daily to Finsbury Park in London. Goods from all parts of the country found their way to Colwick, trains regularly working to and from Peterborough, Whitemoor yard in Cambridgeshire, Liverpool, Sheffield, Hull, Scarborough and Middlesbrough. To power all these trains, shunt wagons, and run local passenger services across the entire GNR system in Nottinghamshire, hundreds of locomotives were stationed at Colwick (16) (no fewer than 250 were recorded there immediately before the First World War) and hundreds of men were employed in all sorts of capacities by the GNR for work in and around Nottingham.

The GNR was not only committed to maintaining and running its own lines in Nottinghamshire, it was also involved with other railways either as joint owner or simply as operator. An example of a line in the first category still clips the very north-east edge of the county on its way between Gainsborough and Doncaster. The GNR had

reached Gainsborough from Lincoln by 1849 but for the next 18 years it ran its Lincoln-Doncaster service over part of the MS&LR's line to Retford. Then from July 1867 GNR trains were diverted onto a new line which branched off the MS&LR immediately west of that company's bridge over the Trent at Gainsborough, passing through new stations at Beckingham, Walkeringham, Misterton (17) and Haxey and Finningley (the latter both in Yorkshire) before reaching Doncaster. Fifteen years later, this section of line (along with the whole of the GNR's 1849 Lincoln-Gainsborough route) was vested in the Great Northern & Great Eastern Joint Railway (GN&GEJR) a company formed in order to prevent the building of a completely new line to connect the Great Eastern Railway (GER) in East Anglia with the collieries in South Yorkshire. By linking together existing lines, the GN&GEJR was able to open up a new through route by the summer of 1882 for the movement of coal southwards between Doncaster and March.

17. Judging by the clean brickwork and a few, slight costume clues, this photograph of the GNR's Misterton station was probably taken within a few years of its opening in 1867. *(Lens of Sutton)*

18. Bingham Road was the first GN&LNWJR station on the line that branched off the Nottingham-Grantham route at Saxondale Junction and headed south-east then southwards into Leicestershire. The station, seen in this amateur Edwardian 'snap' opened on 1st September 1879, the signalbox opened the following year. *(author's collection)*

19. There are so few photographs of regular passenger trains on the Nottingham Suburban Railway that inevitably this image has appeared in print before. It shows a GNR train entering Thorneywood station in 1911 with a train bound for Nottingham Victoria. *(photo: F. Gillford/Kidderminster Railway Museum)*

20. A photograph taken on 29th September 1952 looking east from the footbridge at the GNR's Basford & Bulwell station. The lines straight ahead were part of the GNR's original 1875 route joining the Nottingham-Grantham line at Colwick; the lines diverging to the left were laid in at the end of the 1890s to connect with the GCR main line at Bulwell South Junction whilst immediately under the bridge in the background, two other 1890s connections headed for Bagthorpe Junction on the GCR main line. *(photo: V.R. Webster/Kidderminster Railway Museum)*

By then this was the second joint undertaking entered into by the GNR affecting its services in Nottinghamshire. From the beginning of 1880, London & North Western Railway (LNWR) coal trains began to ply between Welham (just outside Northampton) and Doncaster, and between Welham and Colwick, using a new route through Leicestershire built and operated by the Great Northern & London, North Western Joint Railway (GN&LNWJR). Its route northwards through Leicestershire, diverged at Stathern, one line running due north through Bottesford to join a new GNR branch from there to the main line at Newark, and the other striking north-west to Saxondale (18) where it joined the Nottingham-Grantham line. To handle its traffic to and from the Nottinghamshire coalfield, the LNWR stabled its own locomotives at the GNR's Colwick yard in a new engine shed. Over 60 engines were recorded

there in 1882, whilst adjacent to this new shed the company erected 39 houses in two new terraces for its staff. To cater for all other general goods arriving and departing from Nottingham itself, meanwhile, the LNWR used running powers over the GNR to reach its own impressive brick warehouse built off Manvers Street and opened in the summer of 1888. At Newark much more modest facilities were built by the GNR to house and service a handful of engines for trains up and down its Bottesford branch, on and off the GN&LNWJR and for shunting local sidings.

The Nottingham Suburban Railway (NSR) was an example of an independent company whose line was operated for it by the GNR. Running north-south on the east side of Nottingham it was promoted in the mid-1880s as a predominantly passenger line, not to serve existing communities but in a bold attempt to encourage the development of suburban housing between Daybrook in the north and Sneinton in the south. When finished, the line had the air of a GNR branch provided with that company's latest equipment, the most characteristic being the signals and signalboxes, and worked from its opening in December 1889 by the GNR with its own engines and carriages (19). But the line never fulfilled the aspirations of its promoters, with the few passengers who did use it being won over to Nottingham's electric tram services within a decade.

Far more successful was the GNR's partnership with the MS&LR in the financing, designing and building of Nottingham's fine new central station - Nottingham Victoria - managed by a joint station committee. From 1900 all the GNR's passenger services in and around the city were concentrated on this station. To facilitate this, junctions had been laid to the north of the city at Bulwell (20) and at Bagthorpe (Basford). Similarly, a heavily engineered (and very costly) double track connection bypassing the original Ambergate terminus off London Road had been built to join the new GCR main line at Weekday Cross, just south of Victoria station. The improvements for GNR passengers coming in from the coalfields, from Stafford, Derby, Newark or Grantham on local trains or on expresses from London Kings Cross, via Grantham were immediate (21). At Victoria, they had access to all the latest passenger facilities, could step out straight into the heart of the city or, if they wanted to travel further by train, could patronise GCR services with through carriages to destinations all over the country.

21.   GNR 4-4-0, no. 1360 at the south end of Nottingham Victoria station with the stairs leading to Upper Parliament Street in the background. Photographed in about 1910 this locomotive, sporting its grass or apple green livery had been built in 1899 only a few months before Victoria station opened.
(photo: F. Gillford/R.K. Blencowe Negative Archive)

22. A detail of a postcard sent from Retford to Sheffield in 1907. The photograph shows part of the up platform from where GNR trains departed to Kings Cross as well as MS&LR and later GCR trains to Lincoln, Gainsborough and Grimsby. *(author's collection)*

The passenger facilities at Nottingham Victoria station were not typical of those at other GNR stations in Nottinghamshire. Most country stations remained as they had when first opened with the possible addition of a simple (by 19th century standards) timber waiting room, made to a common design. Such waiting rooms were usually on the platform opposite the original buildings which housed the booking office and Station Master's accommodation. Only at Newark and Retford (22) in the last half of the 19th century were additional brick buildings added and more elaborate canopies erected over platforms to protect passengers from the rain.

The reputation of the GNR was not, however, based on its stations but on the speed of both its goods and passenger services. In the years leading up to the start of the First World War, the company ran some of the fastest passenger express services in the world, beautifully polished teak carriages racing along behind engines painted the colour of spring grass (23). Although the trains have changed, the reputation for speed on the GNR main line still persists, whereas the company's once extensive network of colliery branches and local stations in the rest of the county have vanished.

23.   When this photograph was taken in c.1910, speeds approaching 70mph were achieved here at Scrooby. Steam locomotive no.284, designed and built at Doncaster in 1904, is seen racing southwards to Kings Cross past Scrooby signalbox opened in 1872 (and closed 1924). *(Great Northern Railway Society)*

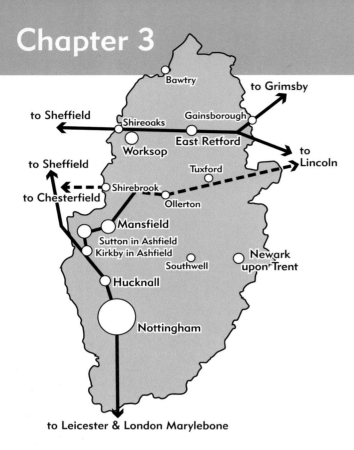

to Grimsby
to Sheffield
Bawtry
Shireoaks
Gainsborough
East Retford
Worksop
to Lincoln
to Sheffield
Tuxford
to Chesterfield
Shirebrook
Ollerton
Mansfield
Sutton in Ashfield
Kirkby in Ashfield
Southwell
Newark upon Trent
Hucknall
Nottingham
to Leicester & London Marylebone

The Manchester, Sheffield & Lincolnshire Railway
(Great Central Railway)

The railway company that was destined to give Nottingham its most impressive main-line passenger station at the very beginning of the 20th century, started its business in the north of the county, quietly, 51 years earlier. The Manchester, Sheffield & Lincolnshire Railway (MS&LR) was formed in 1847 as an amalgamation between the Sheffield, Ashton-under-Lyne & Manchester Railway, which had been running trains between those places since December 1845, and three other companies whose plans were yet to be realised – the Sheffield & Lincolnshire Junction, the Great Grimsby & Sheffield and the Sheffield & Lincolnshire Extension railways. The MS&LR's route through Nottinghamshire from west to east saw it enter the county at Shireoaks, pass through Worksop and Retford before dividing at Clarborough Junction (just east of the 600m/656 yards long tunnel there) one route branching off north-east to cross the River Trent into Lincolnshire at Gainsborough, and heading for Grimsby and

New Holland, and the other route branching south-east to cross the Trent by another bridge into Lincolnshire at Torksey to approach Lincoln from the north-west. This latter route was christened the Leverton Branch and to reach the city, the MS&LR had been obliged by Parliament, during all the 'Railway Mania' business of 1845-6, to share part of the GNR's planned Lincoln to Gainsborough line between Sykes Junction (near Saxilby) and Lincoln.

As with the GNR, the MS&LR opened for goods and passenger traffic in stages. The population of Grimsby and New Holland could patronise MS&LR trains from March 1848 (and reach Lincoln by another MS&LR line from February the following year). What became the main line between Sheffield and the Humber via Shireoaks, Worksop, (24) Retford and Gainsborough, opened for goods and passenger trains on 16th July 1849. Two months later, on the completion of the Doncaster-Retford section of the GNR's main line, that company's trains began to use the MS&LR's Retford station. From there, the GNR had Parliamentary rights to run a service over the MS&LR to Lincoln in the east and Sheffield in the west. At this point in the story, the historical facts vary between three different sources. According to Charles H. Grinling who wrote the first history of the GNR in 1898, the MS&LR's Leverton Branch opened on the same day as the Doncaster-Retford line – 4th September 1849 - enabling trains to carry spectators for Doncaster's Races over GNR tracks between Peterborough, Spalding, Boston and Lincoln and then over the MS&LR's Leverton Branch to Retford and onwards by GNR to Doncaster. John Wrottesley's more recent history of the GNR (1979), however, claims the branch did not open until 7th August 1850 when the MS&LR stopped obstructing the GNR from running a Lincoln-Sheffield service over the line whereas in Volume One of George Dow's history of the Great Central Railway (1959), although giving the same opening date for the Leverton Branch as Wrottesley, that author blames the delay on the

24. Worksop station as it appeared in the immediate pre-First World War years, with a substantial two storey extension to the original 1849 station building added in 1900 very prominent to the left. The new building along with the refurbishment of the existing allowed for two new refreshment rooms, one for first and the other for third class passengers. New waiting rooms were built on the opposite platform at the same time. *(detail from Kingsway Real Photo postcard/author's collection)*

25. A GCR west-bound train negotiating the tight curve at the north end of the GNR's Retford station on 6th May 1935. The connection shown here was part of the 1859 junction improvements made between the MS&LR and GNR lines at Retford. *(photo: E.R. Morten)*

GNR for not allowing the MS&LR to run its trains over part of the GNR's line between Sykes Junction and Lincoln station! If, as seems likely, a dispute did postpone the use of the Leverton Branch then, no matter who was at fault, it was almost certainly due to the influence then being exerted on the MS&LR by the GNR's implacable rival, the London & North Western Railway (LNWR).

Throughout the 19th century, in order to stay in business, the MS&LR was obliged to make alliances with a number of major railway companies, and not always willingly. During the 1850s it was the LNWR and the GNR who shaped the MS&LR's policies, particularly in regard to London traffic. The MS&LR shared a station in Manchester with the LNWR (London Road, now Piccadilly) and as that company had a monopoly of London services from Manchester in the 1840s, all MS&LR passengers travelling to and from the capital were obliged to use LNWR trains. This might not seem relevant to a history of railways in Nottinghamshire, but when the GNR main line was complete throughout between London and Doncaster from the summer of 1852 (crossing as it did the MS&LR at Retford) it would have been possible for MS&LR passengers to travel to London, not from Manchester on LNWR trains, but via Retford on GNR trains. The GNR was keen to encourage this, but due to the LNWR's influence on its weaker colleague, the MS&LR was forced to timetable its trains so they did not make convenient connections at Retford. When relations between the LNWR and the MS&LR cooled slightly, the GNR was quick to make an approach to the MS&LR with the result that from August 1857 the two companies launched through London-Manchester services via Retford that were deliberately timed to match the schedule of LNWR trains. The LNWR retaliated by making it very uncomfortable for MS&LR staff and passengers at Manchester's London Road station, and by cutting its London fares. Parliamentary intervention the following year finally put a stop to the fares war and extreme cases of intimidation that had

occured at Manchester station, and the LNWR was forced to accept that its London-Manchester monopoly was over. In 1859 the physical connections between the MS&LR and the GNR at Retford were improved and from July of that year the former closed its own station running all its trains through that of the GNR (25).

From then until the end of the century, the MS&LR was dependant on the GNR for access to and from London via Retford and although this arrangement was both remunerative and prestigious for both companies, the events of the 1850s undoubtedly influenced the MS&LR's desire to, some day, have its own independent route to London. From July 1883 the Manchester-London, Kings Cross service was accelerated to offer passengers a journey of 4½ hours achieved by the trains only stopping at Sheffield and Grantham en route. The GNR allowed the MS&LR to use its own locomotives between these two places, a practice that continued until the MS&LR opened its own line to London, Marylebone 16 years later.

The MS&LR's quest to build its own line to London began in earnest in the late 1880s and once this ambition became clear to the companies operating the established routes to and from the capital – the LNWR, GNR and MR – the MS&LR had a tough fight on its hands. Over the years it had negotiated with all these companies in order to get to the capital, even trying to get them to cooperate in the building of a new joint railway. Only the arrangement with the GNR had come somewhere near to fulfilling its aspiration so it was ironic that it was to be this company that finally provided the MS&LR with a launch pad for its own, independent mission to London.

In 1889 the MS&LR secured Parliamentary approval for an extension southwards from Beighton (in north Derbyshire) to a junction with the GNR's Leen Valley line at Annesley. From there, the MS&LR ran goods and coal trains into the GNR's Colwick yard from October 1892, and a passenger service in and out of that company's Nottingham, London Road station from the second day of 1893. The MS&LR had promised the GNR that this was the limit of its aspirations but that promise proved to be hollow. Before the line was even open for traffic, the MS&LR was back in Westminster seeking approval for an extension from Annesley, through the heart of Nottingham to Leicester, onwards to Aylesbury linking with the Metropolitan Railway into London and then a short new line into a new terminus at Marylebone. Opposition from the MR and GNR prevented the initial plans from succeeding, but in March 1893 the MS&LR gained its Act of Parliament for the new main line.

The GNR had been bought off by being offered running powers to Manchester and Sheffield and generous connections to its existing lines around Nottingham. This would allow the GNR to run all its services into the MS&LR's new central station at Nottingham with the additional option of contributing to the design, construction and running of the station. It is interesting to note that Sir Edward Parry, who was appointed as the MS&LR's resident engineer for the extension through Nottingham, had, back in 1881, suggested building a central station on what became the site of Nottingham Victoria, into which all passenger services then being operated into the town by the MR, GNR and LNWR could have been connected. Nine years later in 1890 during early negotiations prior to the tabling of the MS&LR's first London Extension Bill, those companies had all been approached again with the same suggestion of participating in a new central station. Once again they had declined. The MR was obviously already too well established in its own location, but the LNWR which was using running powers over the GNR to offer a limited Nottingham-Northampton service into London Road station, could have benefited from switching to a new central station. The LNWR's refusal to contribute towards the MS&LR's station plans probably explains why its Northampton trains continued to rumble in and out of London Road station (Low Level after 1899) when all GNR trains had abandoned that terminus for Victoria. (The Northampton service was not rerouted into Victoria until May 1944!)

The construction of the MS&LR through Nottinghamshire was a massive undertaking and no expense was spared on its infrastructure. Heading south, sheds were constructed adjacent to Annesley Colliery to house 30 locomotives with all the associated servicing and minor repair facilities. A marshalling yard for nearly 2,000 coal wagons was laid out and land purchased to double that capacity if required. Then, after sweeping over the lines of the MR and GNR, and crossing the River Leen at Bulwell on a 384m (420yard) long blue brick viaduct, the main line headed straight for the centre of Nottingham. The contrast between the MS&LR's entry into the county town and the MCR's timid approach 60 years earlier could not have been greater. In 1839 the MCR brought into use a single line from Trent junction terminating in open countryside – The Meadows – well to the south of Nottingham where a station no larger than a smart domestic house was erected. At the end of the century, the MS&LR literally blasted a 5.3 hectare (13 acre) hole in the middle of Britain's newest city (granted that status on 18th June 1897) having already demolished an estimated 1,300 houses, 24 pubs, a church, the Guildhall and the Union Workhouse. Demolition on this scale in Nottingham was not witnessed again until the council slum clearances of the 1930s and then during the road and office blocks building boom of the 1960s when, ironically, Victoria station was one of the many victims.

The MCR's 1839 station had two platforms 48.7m (160ft) long, initially used by five trains a day. Nottingham Victoria when it opened on 24th May 1900, (two years, 9 months after the MS&LR had proudly changed its name to the Great Central Railway (GCR)), boasted 12 platforms, two of which were 400m (almost a quarter of a mile) in length. Into these platforms, 170 passenger trains worked daily.

26. With Upper Parliament Street bridge already in place in the background, some impressive shoring timbers can be seen in this late 1890s photograph supporting Clinton Street, Nottingham.*(NCCLSL)*

27. A London, Marylebone-bound express racing through Ruddington station at the end of the GCR's independent existence. When this photograph was taken, the engine had only just entered traffic, built in 1922 at the GCR's Gorton Works, numbered 5503 and named 'Somme' in memory of that terrible First World War battle. *(photo: G. Coltas)*

South of Victoria station, after threading carefully under Thurland Street (26) to the junction with the GNR at Weekday Cross, a long brick viaduct with steel bridges took the line through Broad Marsh, over the Nottingham Canal and defiantly over the MR's station. When in 1903/4 the MR came to rebuild its 1848 station, it was prevented by these GCR structures from erecting an overall roof as it had when rebuilding Leicester station a few years earlier. At Nottingham it was obliged to slot the canopies and buildings for the new platforms under its rival's bridges. A little further south, the GCR laid out sidings for its goods traffic in and out of the city, with facilities for carriages and locomotives close by. It then optimistically laid in separate goods lines that crossed the Trent parallel to the passenger lines all on impressive and identical steel truss bridges. Of all the decisions made when anticipating future traffic growth, this duplication of bridges over the Trent must have been one of the more questionable. The MR with all its huge tonnage of coal coming out of the Erewash Valley had coped with a double track bridge over the same river for 53 years until 1893 when another was built alongside (another tunnel through Redhill was opened at the same time). Once south of the Trent, the GCR provided stations for the villages of Ruddington (27) and East Leake, and Britain's last main line exited Nottinghamshire just north of Loughborough.

On its new main line the GCR operated short, fast trains and its London services soon established a reputation for speed and punctuality (28). In 1903 the fastest London, Marylebone-Nottingham services were the 13.40 and 15.25 that took 2hrs

28. Not an express, or a cross-country service, just a local train made up of old MS&LR four and six-wheeled carriages with no heating or toilets. The train was pulling away from Bulwell Common station past a crowded yard of coal wagons and heading for Nottingham Victoria when this photograph was taken in the early 1920s. *(author's collection)*

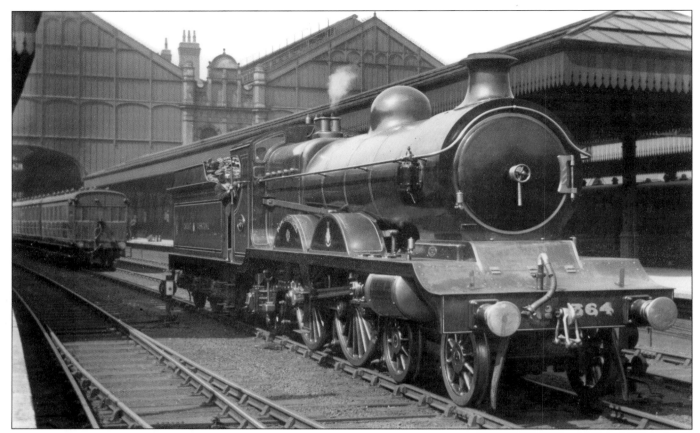

29. Two of the three huge glass and iron screens at the south end of Nottingham Victoria provide an impressive backdrop to GCR 4-4-2, no. 364, 'Lady Henderson'. The beautifully turned out engine with its elaborate livery of Brunswick green, brown, vermilion, black with black and white lining was named after the wife of the GCR's last Chairman. *(photo: F. Gillford/R.K. Blencowe Negative Archive)*

31min to reach Nottingham Victoria. By comparison the MR operated six London, St Pancras-Nottingham expresses taking between 2hrs 22mins and 2hrs 25mins. The following year The GCR introduced the 18.20 from Marylebone that ran non-stop to Nottingham in just 2hrs 13mins. The rivalry continued as by 1910 the best MR times had come down to 2hrs 15mins (for both north- and south-bound services): the GCR being able to offer a 2hrs 21min service.

The GCR did innovate with some interesting cross-country services in collaboration with other railway companies and just before the outbreak of the First World War, passengers from Nottingham Victoria could sit in carriages that would be worked through to Southampton, York, Oxford, Newcastle,

Bournemouth, Aberystwyth, Halifax, Bristol, Huddersfield, Cardiff, Newport, Bath, Winchester, Liverpool, Hull or Yarmouth. Nottingham Victoria station was without a doubt the jewel in the GCR's passenger crown (29), far grander than that provided at Leicester; a structure to rival Marylebone the only other station that boasted signalboxes designed by the architects and not the engineers. Nottingham Victoria was a symbol of the truly great age of the train, a period brought to an end by the First World War and the social consequences of its aftermath.

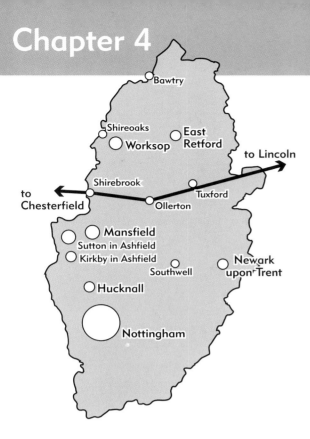

Chapter 4

The Lancashire, Derbyshire & East Coast Railway

As examined in previous chapters, by the 1880s the MR, GNR and MS&LR had a comfortable monopoly in the transportation of Nottinghamshire and Derbyshire coal, the first two companies taking it southwards to London with the MS&LR moving its winnings west into Lancashire, or east to Grimsby. But as exploitation of coal reserves moved towards Mansfield where the MR was unopposed and then was mooted further north-east in Sherwood Forest and 'The Dukeries', not only did the other established companies become eager to expand again, there was also enough incentive for a completely new railway to try its luck in the area.

Unlike today's railway environment where the aspirations of new companies to operate profitable services are decided by successful franchise bidding, Victorian railway companies did not have this option. As mentioned previously, they often negotiated running rights over each other's routes, but the only way a completely new organisation

could compete for traffic was to build new lines. As this was an expensive exercise it was usually confined to existing, well established railways. By the 1880s there were very few challenges from new companies but, at the end of that decade, when the MS&LR was looking to extend southwards towards London and the GNR was keen to extend its Leen Valley line northwards, a scheme was introduced for a new and independent west-east railway connecting the Manchester Ship Canal (then under construction, opening in 1894), to a new port at Sutton-on-Sea on the Lincolnshire coast. One of its specific aims was to serve any new collieries that were opened in Nottinghamshire's Sherwood Forest and 'The Dukeries'. The ambitious plans were submitted by one of the very last brand new railway concerns of the Victorian railway era - the Lancashire, Derbyshire & East Coast Railway (LD&ECR).

The LD&ECR's optimistic aim was borne in part out of the GNR's reluctance to help build and operate the Newark & Ollerton Railway that had gained Parliamentary consent in 1887 for a line branching off the GNR's main line at Muskham. When the hope of channelling 'Dukeries' coal down the GNR's main line faded, investors looked to form another new company. The result was the LD&ECR which successfully secured Parliamentary approval in 1891 to raise £5m for almost 322km (200 miles) of new line across the centre of England.

Despite the apparent optimism, however, the bitter truth was that it was too late in railway history for the establishment of another independent 'coast to coast' main line - especially one that had to cut across the grain of the country through hills and across valleys. The 799.7m (2,624ft) long tunnel under Bolsover (in Derbyshire) proved expensive and difficult to construct; the Trent had to be crossed near Fledborough with a four span steel bridge approached on either side by long brick viaducts totalling nearly 610m (2,000ft); and there were numerous other bridges and viaducts to be made. Sufficient funds for the whole project were not forthcoming and so only the central section

30. LD&ECR 0-4-4T, no.18 built for the railway company by Kitson & Co of Leeds in 1898 photographed at
Edwinstowe station on a west-bound train. The MR engine in the background is on a Mansfield train. Its long
10.5 mile journey via Shirebrook Junction which took about half an hour was made redundant when the
Mansfield Railway started to run passenger trains via its more direct route in 1917 a journey between Mansfield
and Edwinstowe then taking no longer than 17 minutes. *(photo Locomotive & General Railway Photographs;
5867)*

31. Part of the LD&ECR's locomotive works at Tuxford where originally nearly 130 men were employed in the repair
and maintenance of engines and rolling stock. Most prominent are the 'sheer legs' for hoisting large parts such as
boilers from locomotive frames. To the left of these are two steam engine boilers from a Sheffield firm and next to
them, two four-wheeled passenger carriages, which had been bought second-hand from the Great Eastern
Railway. *(photo: Locomotive Publishing Co.)*

between Chesterfield and Pyewipe Junction on the GN&GEJR just west of Lincoln, and a branch from Langwith Junction (later renamed Shirebrook North) to Beighton (just south of Sheffield), were built. It had opened throughout to passengers and freight by the first week of March 1897 (30).

The LD&ECR had looked to other railway companies to help complete its line. Obviously, the MS&LR was not going to support a rival cross-country railway and by the mid-1890s it was preoccupied with fulfilling its long-held aspiration to have its own route to London. The GNR had already declined to become involved with the Newark & Ollerton Railway and probably regretted its existing commitments with the London & North Western Railway (LNWR) and the Great Eastern Railway (GER) in joint railway ventures. It was also running the Nottingham Suburban Railway, and having made a start on its own Leen Valley extension, had no appetite to support another undertaking. The MR, meanwhile, stood back leaving only the GER prepared to inject capital into

the LD&ECR project but only because it was interested in the central section of the line. The GER had manoeuvred the GNR into joining it in operating a route from March to Doncaster via Lincoln (see Chapter Two) which, by giving access to the Yorkshire coalfield, had benefited it more than its partner. With the LD&ECR making a connection with the GN&GEJR west of Lincoln, the GER saw the opportunity to use the central section of the new line as a means of tapping into the lucrative Nottinghamshire coalfield. The GER had no aspirations to reach any further west, so consequently LD&ECR trains never reached the Manchester Ship Canal, and with interests already in other east coast ports, the GER was not going to support Sutton-on-Sea as a new North Sea outlet.

Despite having to rely on the GER's qualified support, the LD&ECR was, nevertheless, optimistic about its future independence. Almost midway between Chesterfield and Lincoln, it bought a large piece of land at Tuxford where it erected facilities to build locomotives (31), although it

32. Dukeries Junction station photographed about 1920 looking south with the GNR main line to the right. This footpath, half a mile from the nearest road to Tuxford, was the only access to the station. All LD&ECR passenger trains running between Chesterfield and Lincoln stopped here and at the company's Tuxford station, compared with only a selection of GNR local trains, that company being more interested in maintaining a service to and from its own Tuxford station (43). (author's collection)

33. Warsop Main Colliery photographed a few years before the First World War. It was operated by the Staveley Coal & Iron Co. Two of the company's wagons are visible in the yard along with large piles of wooden pit props. *(author's collection)*

never did. The works became the centre for maintaining the company's fleet of 37 steam locomotives, 64 passenger carriages and 1,221 goods and coal wagons. It was at Tuxford, too, that the LD&ECR made a physical connection with the GNR main line and generous exchange sidings were constructed, the GNR being granted rights to run its own trains from there to Chesterfield. Where the LD&ECR line bridged the GNR, an interchange station was erected and christened Dukeries Junction (32) to advertise the company's passenger aspirations of attracting tourist traffic. With the prospect of more coalmining in 'The Dukeries', it must always have been a hopeless aim.

Although the LD&ECR was keen to assert its independence, it was inevitable, given its difficult financial position that it should have to allow connections to be made with other lines. The first new link was with the MR immediately north of Shirebrook station on that company's Mansfield-Worksop line. Opened in 1899 the new south to east junction allowed the MR to run passenger trains between Mansfield, Edwinstowe and Ollerton. Another connection with the MR outside the county opened in the following year enabling it to consolidate services in and out of Sheffield at the expense of the MS&LR. By then the MS&LR had changed its name to the Great Central Railway (GCR) on completion of its ambitious main line to London through Nottingham. As stated above, the GNR, whose acquiescence to this new Yorkshire-London line had been achieved by offering it a partnership in the operation of Nottingham Victoria station and running powers through Annesley Tunnel, took advantage of the latter to extend its Leen Valley line northwards to a junction with the LD&ECR in Derbyshire at Langwith, the through route completed in 1901. Langwith Junction became a busy place reflecting the growth of mining communities and the movement of coal from the new pits at Warsop Colliery (1893-8) (33), Shirebrook Colliery (Derbyshire) (1896-7), Sherwood Colliery (1902-3) and Mansfield Colliery (1904-5).

34. Nottingham Road, Mansfield, looking south towards the tram terminus. The plate girder bridge was part of the Mansfield Railway's route through the town whilst visible in the background is the 1871 MR stone bridge that was part of the route to Southwell and Rolleston Junction. *('Milton Series' postcard/author's collection)*

35. Mansfield Central station looking east. Although it is not at all obvious in this view, the station was perched on a high embankment with access from the appropriately named Great Central Road close to its junction with what is now the A6191. *(author's collection)*

Whilst the GER had been holding the financial strings and the MR and GNR had been making their connections with the LD&ECR, the GCR had seemed disinterested. But in 1907, exactly ten years after the rival west-east route had been completed, it absorbed the company. Once that had been achieved, it took its revenge on the MR for using a connection with the LD&ECR to run trains to and from Sheffield and championed the aspirations of the independent Mansfield Railway reviving LD&ECR plans to build a new line to that town in order to break the MR monopoly there. Now it was the turn of the GCR to chase the coal aiming with this new branch to reach the existing Mansfield Colliery, and those planned at Rufford (sunk in 1911 but not operational until 1915) and Clipstone (sunk 1912 but not productive until 1922). Worked by the GCR, the Mansfield Railway branched off the former LD&ECR at Clipstone, (coal trains running by the summer of 1913), passed south of Mansfield town centre (34), and ended in a junction with the GCR's main line at Kirkby South Junction where the GNR Leen Valley Extension also made its connection. The line was completed as a through route by the summer of 1916 with passenger trains between Ollerton and Nottingham Victoria starting to run the following year. This service offered the fastest journeys between Mansfield (35) and Nottingham compared with those run by the MR. In the GCR's last year of independence (1922) eleven Mansfield Central-Nottingham Victoria trains, with 12 in the opposite direction, completed their journeys every weekday in between 30 and 46 minutes. By contrast most of the 16 MR Leen Valley trains between Nottingham and Mansfield took just under an hour, with those into the city being only slightly faster.

The LD&ECR's brief period of independence had been diverting, but by the time the Mansfield Railway opened the balance of railway power in Nottinghamshire had once again been restored. By then, the GCR had completed its developments at Immingham to replace Grimsby as its East Coast dock at the eastern end of its original cross-country line, and Sutton-on-Sea, the LD&ECR's intended port target, had turned its attention to the needs of hundreds of holidaymakers arriving in GNR trains from Nottinghamshire and the East Midlands.

Despite having such a short life as an independent concern, the LD&ECR's line through Nottinghamshire did fulfil some of the aspirations of its original promoters. In 1912 a new deep coal mine was sunk at Welbeck, and by 1915 when that colliery went into production, its coal was being channelled onto the former LD&ECR. In 1923, the year the GCR was absorbed into the London & North Eastern Railway (LNER), work started on another new colliery at Ollerton, and barely two years later shafts were sunk for the new Thorseby Colliery, a mile east of Edwinstowe. Coal from both these pits was fed onto the former LD&ECR. In the same year Thorseby was being developed, a branch line was driven southwards to serve the new Bilsthorpe Colliery that wound its first coal in 1927. The Mansfield Railway too proved its worth in the same period. In 1923 work began on sinking shafts to extract coal at Blidworth, and the railway connection to this colliery ran southwards from New Clipstone. Three decades later, access to the former LD&ECR line influenced the location of what turned out to be Nottinghamshire last new colliery, Bevercotes, sunk in 1958 close to the A1 road south of Retford.

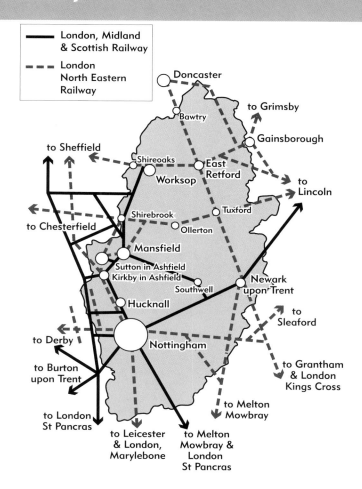

Chapter 5

Legend:
— London, Midland & Scottish Railway
--- London North Eastern Railway

Map locations: Doncaster, to Grimsby, Bawtry, Gainsborough, to Sheffield, Shireoaks, East Retford, Worksop, to Lincoln, to Chesterfield, Shirebrook, Tuxford, Ollerton, Mansfield, Sutton in Ashfield, Kirkby in Ashfield, Newark upon Trent, Southwell, Hucknall, to Sleaford, to Derby, Nottingham, to Burton upon Trent, to Grantham & London Kings Cross, to London St Pancras, to Melton Mowbray, to Leicester & London, Marylebone, to Melton Mowbray & London St Pancras

The London, Midland & Scottish and London North Eastern Railways

In Nottinghamshire – as in the rest of the country - the years between 1839 and 1899 had witnessed the continual expansion of the railway network. Railway managers had justified the building of new lines in two fundamental ways. The first, and most obvious, was based on the assumption that new lines would open up new markets and bring in more profits for the company. The second was that promoting new routes was important as a means of trying to prevent rivals infiltrating existing markets and, whether or not the lines were actually built, the threat would often bring a rival to the negotiation table. If competing railways could not be stopped then duplication and triplication of railway facilities had been viewed by the Victorian managers simply as the manifestation of natural,

healthy capitalist enterprise. Errors of judgement had been made (for example the completion of the MR's Bennerley and Bulwell line as a through route in 1879, only to be truncated west of Kimberley in 1917) but these had been masked by the overall profitability of the companies.

This expansionist philosophy and inter-company manoeuvring is well illustrated by what happened around Kirkby-in-Ashfield and Sutton-in-Ashfield in the ten years between 1888 and 1898. The lines involved have already been examined in previous chapters, but it is very illuminating when they are seen in a wider context as pawns in a political railway game.

In 1888 the MS&LR had announced it was looking to head south from Beighton in Derbyshire with a new line running close to Kirkby-in-Ashfield to join the GNR at Annesley. The following year it entered negotiations with that company because, despite public denials, it was well aware the GNR suspected Annesley to be the springboard for its new route to London, an ambition the GNR would seek to thwart. As the two companies exchanged correspondence, the MR was busily getting approval for a new route through nearby Sutton-in-Ashfield, and in 1889 Parliament granted permission for both the MS&LR Beighton-Annesley extension and the MR scheme. A few months after these approvals the MS&LR made public its intention to extend from Annesley to London, and in direct retaliation the GNR revealed it was seeking permission to extend its Leen Valley line northwards from Annesley to Langwith. As soon as the MR discovered these GNR plans would give Sutton-in-Ashfield a more central station, it abandoned its original scheme and in July 1890 got another Act of Parliament for a short branch from its own Leen Valley line to a terminal station closer to Sutton-in-Ashfield town centre. In 1891 the MS&LR London Extension project failed to secure Parliamentary approval and, having served its political purpose, the GNR withdrew its Leen Valley extension plan. The MR, however, pushed ahead with its Sutton branch and, responding to

36. An Edwardian view of the MR's Sutton Junction station. Until the terminus near the town centre was opened in 1893, this was the original Sutton-in-Ashfield station. At the time the photograph was taken there were 18 passenger trains arriving from and 16 departing to Nottingham daily on weekdays, with an extra two from and three to the city on Saturdays and two each way on Sundays. Journeys took between 24 and 48 minutes. *(author's collection)*

37. The GNR's station serving Sutton-in-Ashfield. Compared with the service from the MR's Sutton Junction, before the First World War the GNR ran nine trains each way between Nottingham (Victoria) and Sutton. The fastest went via the GCR main line (28 minutes), some via the Nottingham Suburban line taking about 45 minutes, and the rest via Gedling taking just under an hour. *(Lens of Sutton)*

this and the realisation that it could no longer oppose the MS&LR's scheme that was resubmitted to Parliament in 1892, the GNR reintroduced its Leen Valley extension plan in the same session. That received its Act in June and only four months later in October the Beighton extension opened for goods traffic. In January the following year passenger trains started to use this route calling at the new station of Kirkby & Pinxton (renamed Kirkby Bentinck in 1925); in March the MS&LR secured its Act of Parliament for the London Extension and in May the MR's new terminal station in Sutton-in-Ashfield opened for passengers (36). A little less than five years later in April 1898, GNR passenger trains started to call at that company's new station in Sutton-in-Ashfield (37) on the Leen Valley extension. There is no better example of how Victorian railway politics worked than this sudden rash of new lines around Kirkby-in-Ashfield and Sutton-in-Ashfield.

Perhaps fittingly, the area was also the location of Nottinghamshire's last new passenger carrying railway. As noted in the previous chapter, the Mansfield Railway had been promoted privately but was, from the outset, supported and operated by the GCR. Passenger trains started to run in April 1917, the new line providing Mansfield with its second station, Kirkby-in-Ashfield with its third (38), and Sutton-in-Ashfield with its fourth. Although Mansfield councillors could finally celebrate an end to the MR's 68 year monopoly in the town, elsewhere railway companies had been forced to make economies. As the First World War dragged on some stations were made the subject of temporary closures – and one that had lost its passenger service only three months before the Mansfield Railway opened was the MR's terminal station in Sutton-in-Ashfield!

38.   Kirkby-in-Ashfield station on the Mansfield Railway looking north. Although this photograph was taken just after midday on 31 December 1955 (the last day of a regular passenger service) the station had changed little since it opened. *(photo: J.P. Wilson)*

39. Nottingham Victoria station with the station hotel to the right, just part of a familiar, busy city scene in the early 1920s. *(postcard, C.& A.G. Lewis, 'Colonial Series'/author's collection)*

The Mansfield Railway was the last of its type, because by the time it opened all the country's railway companies had accepted that there were almost no opportunities left for network expansions that would generate sufficient returns on any initial investment. Already, emphasis in management thinking had shifted from the building of new lines to the improvement of services and facilities on existing routes. In the years leading up to the outbreak of the First World War better carriages with improved facilities for all classes of passenger had appeared, faster services were introduced, and the growth in the provision of through carriages between far-flung places, holiday excursions, and special tours were all examples of this refocusing of priorities. Looking at the last pre-war timetables with their copious notes and advertisements, you get the feeling that travelling was almost an end in itself; that reaching ones destination was almost equally important as how

well one travelled, how comfortable were the seats or how good the meals, and, particularly for First Class travellers, how subservient the railway staff were en route. In 2010 we use trains to get from A to B as quickly and as comfortably as possible; perhaps unlike the Edwardian traveller, we do not expect to be pampered along the way.

The First World War marked the end of the great 'railway age' when autonomous companies had determined where railways were to be built, how they were run and what services and facilities should be provided. For a number of years prior to the outbreak of hostilities there had been those who argued that because the business decisions of railways had been driven purely by competition, the results were unnecessary replication of services and facilities actually working to the detriment of a genuinely public railway service. The tangle of routes and over provision of stations around

40. On Vernon Road a woman steps out in front of a tram headed for the city centre in the first decade of the twentieth century. As with so many Edwardian images reproduced in this book, we have to remember that the photographer captured something that was brand new at the time. Electric trams had started running on this route in the summer of 1901, their frequency and convenience immediately reducing the number of people using the adjacent MR's Leen Valley line. *(author's collection)*

41. Also on the MR's Leen Valley line was Bulwell station, photographed in July 1948. In 1900 before electric trams started to run between the city and Bulwell, 138,000 passengers used the railway station. In 1902, the first full year of competing directly with the tram service, that figure had dropped to just under 84,000. *(photo: W.A. Camwell)*

Kirkby-in-Ashfield and Sutton-in-Ashfield already mentioned illustrate this view perfectly.

Edwardian management attitudes were noticeably different from those of their predecessors. In a move away from the antagonism and fierce competition that had characterised Victorian railway politics, by 1909 the GNR, GCR and GER were optimistic about a proposed amalgamation. The companies might have been ready to co-operate more intimately but their Parliamentary bill was withdrawn as the debates at Westminster strayed into contentious talks about nationalisation. It was not until all the country's railways had been placed under direct Government control during the First World War that such fundamental changes became acceptable to an increasing number of politicians. Full nationalisation did not materialise after the War, however, and instead it was agreed to group the railway companies into four large conglomerates in an effort to encourage some in-house rationalisation. This 'grouping' of the railways came into effect on 1st January 1923 with the GNR, GCR and GER being finally brought together and joining with the larger and more powerful North Eastern Railway (NER).

By 1923 there was no one left alive who could remember a time before railways. The novelty of the 1830s and 40s was folk memory. Though comparatively new, Nottingham Victoria station had rapidly become part of the urban environment in a bustling city (39). After the war there was no appetite, or funds, for new grand stations and local councillors were no longer interested in lobbying railways to provide better facilities. Railways were taken for granted, having become just part of the landscape. In the depressed economy of the late 1920s and 30s it was enough of a challenge to make the constituent parts of the new railway 'groups' work together without trying to implement completely new policies. In Nottinghamshire there was little to indicate the railways were under

different management and gradually, certain parts of the network and certain time-honoured practises began to appear 'old-fashioned'.

Throughout the inter-war period, railways remained the best means of making long distance journeys for both people and goods. For shorter trips, however, there was increasingly more choice and it was in this market that the first significant contraction of railway services started to be made. Nottingham's trams had already robbed the railways of hundreds of passengers in the immediate pre-First World War years (40), so it was natural that commuters turned to the brand-new motor and trolley buses when they were introduced in the 1920s. The MR's Lenton station had closed due to competition from trams as early as June 1911 as passenger numbers evaporated from just over 14,000 in 1907 to a little short of 2,500 three years later. Less dramatic, but still noticeable, were falls recorded at the MR's stations at Basford, Radford and Bulwell (41) - but not as yet sufficient for management to consider closing them completely. With the MR grouped into the new London, Midland & Scottish Railway (LMS) along with the LNWR in 1923, further cuts might have been expected, but the new company was very cautious. It dithered in regard to the Sutton-in-Ashfield branch, first closing it to passengers in 1917, reopening it in September 1923, only to suspend the service less than three years later in May 1926 before finally relenting four months later. (The passenger service finally went in 1949). The LMS did withdraw its passenger service between Southwell and Mansfield from August 1929 replacing it with a bus service, but there were other priorities at work here (see below) and elsewhere on former MR lines little else changed.

Grouped into the London North Eastern Railway (LNER), along with the GNR, the GCR was the first to feel the effects of rationalisation under new management. Carrington station (42), just north of Nottingham Victoria was closed in 1928 with

42. Carrington station looking north on 2nd September 1962. A year after this station had opened in 1899, Nottingham Corporation recorded that it had siphoned people away from the horse-drawn tram service. This situation was quickly reversed when the tram route was electrified and after trolley buses and motor buses started running along Mansfield Road, the station's days were really numbered. *(photo: J. Marshall/Kidderminster Railway Museum)*

43. Staff happy to pose for the camera at the GNR's Tuxford station in the early 1920s. *(author's collection)*

Bulwell Hall Halt (opened in 1909) closing two years later. In the summer of 1931, meanwhile, Checker House station, halfway between Worksop and Retford, was closed to passengers. After that, no further economies were made in ex-GCR services. Deeper cuts were made, however, on ex-GNR lines. From September 1931 all six stations on the ex-GNR Leen Valley line (including its 1901 extension) were closed to passengers (Bulwell Forest had closed two years earlier) leaving all services concentrated on those of the former GCR. In the same month Scrooby, on the main line between Retford and Doncaster, closed and passenger trains ceased running over the Nottingham Suburban Railway.

It is difficult to assess how effective these cuts were, and it was probably difficult for the railway companies to calculate what the savings might be compared to the potential losses of closing stations or removing trains from the timetable. Nevertheless, looking objectively at the inter-war period, there is no doubt that some further rationalisation could have been achieved without incurring customer hardship or resentment. For example, LNER trains continued to stop at Dukeries Junction, Tuxford, both on the main line and on the former LD&ECR, despite the fact that services to exactly the same destinations were offered from the other two stations in the town (43) – stations, moreover, which, unlike Dukeries Junction, could be reached by road. In Nottingham, the LNER inexplicably continued the tradition of its predecessor (the GNR) in allowing LMS (ex-LNWR) trains to and from Northampton into its London Road (Low Level) station (44). It is still difficult to understand why these trains were not diverted to Victoria until after the Second

44. Former LNWR 2-4-0 no. 1674, 'Delhi', renumbered 5020 by its new owner the LMS in 1927, departing from Nottingham London Road Low Level station with a train for Northampton sometime before 1930 (when the engine was scrapped). The first and last carriages were still in LNWR livery when this photograph was taken. *(Stephenson Locomotive Society)*

45. A Nottingham Victoria-Derby (Friargate) train has just pulled away from New Basford station on the former GCR main line in the mid-1930s. The wooden carriages are forty year old ex-GNR stock. On the left are the railway carriage sheds. *(photo: A.B. Crompton)*

World War when the expense of maintaining passenger facilities at the old Ambergate terminus could finally be eradicated.

Although the LNER had sensibly rearranged its Leen Valley passenger service in 1931, it still left places such as Hucknall with two stations run by rival companies. And as neither the LMS or LNER was going to close its station to benefit the other, and with more passengers being tempted away to bus services in the 1930s, both railway companies found themselves dividing falling receipts between them. The same dilemma faced the two companies in relation to Newark-Nottingham passenger services that, logically, could have been concentrated on just one route. The LNER service via Cotham - a station where less than 550 tickets had been sold in 1936 netting the company a mere £29 – remained stubbornly in place until the 1950s.

Some later analysts have argued that piecemeal closures and the withdrawal of passenger services were not the best ways to make savings, and that railways ought to have looked at more fundamental ways to produce economies. Between the wars almost every station in the county was fully staffed, and most had a resident Station Master. Most signalboxes (and there were hundreds in the county) were manned continuously either on a two or three shift pattern. Every level crossing had to have staff in attendance if there was no supervising signalbox, and many of those staff lived in railway cottages alongside those crossings. It was not until the 1960s that economies here were possible with the introduction of unmanned crossings with 'continental barriers' (as they were disparagingly termed at the time). But in the 1920s and 30s, changes like this were not considered and economies in how the surviving local passenger services were operated were minimal. Unlike the LMS, the LNER never substituted buses for trains in Nottinghamshire, only replacing the traditional combination of steam locomotive and carriages with single carriage steam railcars on a few very local city services. Elsewhere, wooden pre-grouping carriages continued to bounce passengers between local stations (45). There would have been very little difference between a local train of 1923 and one of 1939 whereas on the roads, the open-sided charabanc of 1923 with solid tyres and a maximum speed of under 30mph, was an amusing historical curiosity by 1939, superseded by fully-enclosed, comfortable buses all capable of breaking the 1935 30mph 'built-up' area speed limit. This comparison was perhaps not so important in country areas where the railway had less competition. In and around Barnstone (46), for example, where five trains a week could take you to Nottingham or Melton Mowbray in about

half an hour in either direction. For those in the city, however, buses were cleaner, more convenient and the obvious choice if you did not own your own car.

Where the railways did maintain their market was in the provision of long distance services, both passenger and freight. As well as the glamour associated with trains such as 'The Flying Scotsman' (47) or 'The Silver Jubilee' running along its East Coast main line, the LNER also maintained a certain prestige (albeit no longer in terms of speed), in the variety of cross-country services it offered from Nottingham Victoria station. Inherited from the GCR, the 'Ports to Ports' train continued to run, timed to cover the distance between Cardiff and Nottingham Victoria in four and a half hours and onwards to Newcastle in a further four hours. The GCR's Aberdeen-Penzance service was also preserved, although you needed a

46.   A Nottingham-Northampton train at Barnstone station on 16th September 1937. Although a mute record, this photograph does show the former MR 4-4-0 no.510 blowing off quite fiercely, the sound adding a little urgency to an otherwise tranquil scene. *(photo: R.A. Wheeler)*

47.   The non-stop Edinburgh-London, Kings Cross 'Flying Scotsman' train hauled by 4-6-2 no.2796 'Spearmint' passing through Crow Park station in the mid-1930s. Serving Sutton-on-Trent this station opened in 1882 and in 1936 sold 3,034 3rd class and 4 first class tickets. *(photo: H. Gordon Tidey)*

very good reason for occupying the same carriage for upto nine hours if travelling from Nottingham Victoria to the Cornish coast.

Holiday traffic was another area where the railways continued to hold their own. The GNR had given many Nottinghamshire people their first glimpse of the sea when the routes to Skegness, Mablethorpe and Sutton-on-Sea were completed in 1873, 1877 and 1888 respectively, and the LNER happily continued to carry the annual summer exodus to the east coast from Nottingham and the coalfield towns. A trip to Skegness just before the war by the fastest summer Fridays and Saturdays only train (the 6pm from Nottingham Victoria) was timetabled to take just one minute over two hours. Also linking the county with the same coast, but with the towns of Cromer, Yarmouth or Lowestoft, holiday makers could travel on Midland & Great Northern Joint Railway (M&GNJR) trains from Nottingham's LMS station (48). By the outbreak of

the Second World War even though the company had been transferred completely into the hands of the LNER, its trains continued to use the same station and cover the same route, a trip between Nottingham and Yarmouth occupying four and a half hours by the fastest Manchester-Lowestoft service. Using its own trains, the LMS could offer summer Saturday through carriages to and from Paignton, Torquay, Bournemouth, Morecombe, Blackpool or the Welsh coast.

Going on holiday by train is now a distant memory as is another aspect of railway operations which was taken for granted in 1920s and 30s - the movement of freight by rail (49). Between the wars this brought in more income for the LMS and LNER in Nottinghamshire than passenger traffic. Anyone could take items to almost any station in the county as well as agents in the larger communities and pay for them to be sent by rail to their destination. In the majority of towns, the

48. The yellow ochre livery of this M&GNJR locomotive must have glowed in the sunshine when photographed at Nottingham (MR) station on 10th August 1935. When the LNER assumed full control of the M&GNJR the following year, all the locomotives it inherited were painted black. *(photo: G.A. Barlow)*

49. A crowded goods yard, a scene that would have been familiar all over Nottinghamshire and elsewhere in the country in the 1920s and 30s. This particular view was taken by the official MR photographer on 31st March 1922 in part of Nottingham's extensive goods sidings stretching for a mile west of the station. *(National Railway Museum: detail from official MR photograph DY12476)*

railways collected from and delivered to clients using their own road vehicles, mostly horse-drawn. Packages were either transported by passenger train or via the 'pick-up' goods that took them on to larger stations or marshalling yards such as Colwick where they were transferred to other trains. It soon became apparent, however, that goods travelling less than 32km (20 miles) between dispatch and destination could be handled much more effectively (and cheaply) by road hauliers.

Railways, however, did manage to hang on to business from firms that had physical connections with the network. At the Grouping there were 65 colliery sidings and just over 150 private railway sidings in Nottinghamshire serving gas works, maltings, wagon works, gypsum quarries, timber yards and glue works and other more specialist businesses. One such was the Hathern Station Brick and Terracotta Works, located at the southernmost tip of the county, and reliant on its connection to the former MCR main line for the reception of coal for its kilns and for dispatching its architectural building components for new banks, pubs, town halls, swimming baths, shops and hotels being erected all over the country and in Northern Ireland. Whereas passenger stations were closing between the wars, the number of private sidings actually increased. For example, when Britain's second sugar beet factory was opened outside Newark in 1921 it was located to take full advantage of connections to the River Trent and the Nottingham-Lincoln line. A similar riverside location with rail access was chosen for Nottinghamshire's other sugar beet factory completed in 1924 on the newly established Nottingham Colwick Estates, south of the city. The site, with a connection to the Nottingham-Grantham line, had been developed in 1917 to stimulate new industry. It achieved its aims and attracted firms dealing in bulky raw materials including a number handling oils and petroleum spirits.

Nottinghamshire was fortunate between the wars in being somewhat cushioned from the worst effects of global depression by the expansion of newer industries (such as those mentioned above) as well as pharmaceuticals and cycle and cigarette manufacture. The coal-mining industry was still growing as well and, therefore, continuing to provide traditional, heavy industrial employment opportunities. In fact it was the opening of new pits at Ollerton (sunk 1923), Blidworth (1926) and Blisthorpe (1927) that brought significant investment by the LMS and LNER in new lines purely for coal traffic. Jointly funded, a single track line from Ollerton joining the LMS Southwell-Mansfield line at Farnsfield was opened in 1931, the passenger service on the latter route having been withdrawn two years earlier. At the same time a new connection was brought into use between the Southwell-Mansfield and Nottingham-Lincoln lines at Fiskerton thereby completing an alternative route for coal emanating from the new collieries avoiding Mansfield, Kirkby-in-Ashfield, and the congested Erewash Valley line. Via this route, loaded wagons were received into a much enlarged yard at Beeston, west of Nottingham, upgraded as part of the same scheme.

By the end of the 1930s, with war looming, it was even more important to ensure that coal transport was handled as efficiently as possible. Belatedly, in the summer of 1938 the LMS began modernising the way empty coal wagons were dealt with in Toton yard. The operation of points and mechanical 'retarders' was controlled centrally, speeding up the process of wagon sorting previously done by shunters on the ground. Although planned at the same time, the upgrading of the eastern side of the complex at Toton – the up yard – where loaded wagons arrived from the collieries, had to wait until peace returned.

Chapter 6

British Railways

1945-1955 : Business as usual

The railways of Nottinghamshire, as everywhere else in the country, emerged from the Second World War, both frailer and dirtier. (50). Nationalisation of the network in 1948 brought with it optimism, different liveries, new station suffixes, but little else (see Table 3). Lines once operated by the LMS were placed under British Railways, London Midland Region (LMR) management, whilst those run by the LNER fell into British Railways Eastern Region (ER) hands. Gradually a few new engines (51) and carriages appeared, but fundamentally, nothing changed. Staff loyalties and working conditions remained as before; steam engines, old and new, continued to haul passenger and goods trains, mostly running to slower schedules than before the war. The mechanisation of Toton up yard was completed, but after that, there was no further large-scale investment in Nottinghamshire's infrastructure. For some later analysts, the period between 1945 and 1955 was one of missed opportunities.

Attempts to nationalise the road haulage industry and integrate all land transport were finally abandoned by the returning Conservative administration in 1951 and with improvements to bus services and the relentless increase in private car ownership, the railways continued to lose business to roads. The railway's response in Nottinghamshire, as it had been before the war, was station closures and the withdrawal of passenger services.

The LMS had closed Edwalton station to passengers in July 1941 during the war, and Pinxton & Selston station to regular passenger services in July 1947. Four months into British Railway ownership, in May 1948, the former MR (LMS) station at Upper Broughton was closed, with its neighbours Widmerpool and Plumtree

succumbing in February the following year. Seven months later, in September 1949, the former LMS Sutton-in-Ashfield branch finally closed to passengers and then in October 1951 to goods. Two months after that, passenger trains stopped travelling between Chesterfield and Langwith Junction (Shirebrook North) on the former LD&ECR. The service between there and Lincoln (serving the stations at Warsop, Edwinstowe, Ollerton (52), Boughton, Tuxford Central, Fledborough, Clifton-on-Trent, Doddington & Harby and Skellingthorpe in Lincolnshire) lasted a little longer until September 1955. Dukeries Junction station on that route had closed in March 1950, and was followed in the space of eight years by the loss of all the other villages stations on the former LNER, East Coast main line.

1955-1962 : A flicker of modernisation

As the pace of change in society accelerated, British Railways caught the spirit of the times and in 1955 unveiled its Modernisation Plan. Massive investment was promised including the electrification of the former GNR main line through Newark and Retford. It all seemed very positive. On the ground in Nottinghamshire the effects were varied. The elimination of steam trains was a key aim of the Plan, and the ER was quick to introduce diesel multiple units (DMUs – ancestors of all passenger trains operating at the beginning of the 21st century) between Nottingham Victoria and Grantham (53) in September of that year*.

This positive investment in Nottinghamshire's railways was balanced by the loss of passenger services elsewhere. From January 1956, it was no longer possible to travel between Nottingham Victoria and Mansfield Central when the regular service of seven southbound and eight northbound trains was withdrawn. Although Kirkby-in-Ashfield, Sutton-in-Ashfield and Mansfield stations on this route remained open for holiday excursions a little longer, any objective assessment has to conclude that all these communities were no worse off than

50. The refreshment room between platforms 4 and 5 at Nottingham (MR) photographed in 1957. There is probably no better image of how depressing railways could be for passengers in that decade, although railway enthusiasts who were train spotters at the time, have different views.
(photo: British Railways, LMR 57/24)

51. One of British Railways new 'standard' steam locomotives, no 84006 built at Crewe in 1953, approaches Beeston station with a Railway Correspondence & Travel Society rail tour on 24th September 1955. For railway enthusiasts, the 1950s were the age of the rail tour when train spotting was almost every boy's favourite hobby. *(photo: R.J. Buckley)*

52.   Former GCR 4-6-2T, no.69812 takes on water at Ollerton station in the 1950s whilst heading a Lincoln Central-Shirebrook North service.

53.   One of the DMUs that replaced steam trains on the Nottingham Victoria-Grantham passenger services from 1955. This one was photographed approaching Aslockton station from the east on 13th July 1963. On the right is the large brick goods warehouse once vital for both the community and the railway but, by the time this photograph was taken, it had only a year left before closure (and eventual demolition). *(photo: H.B. Priestley/NL&CSLSL 85936/85)*

before, still having access to timetabled services over the ex-MR Leen Valley line in and out of Nottingham.

In 1958, the former GCR main line through Nottingham Victoria was transferred from the ER to the LMR who, being already responsible for two routes between Nottingham and London, were unlikely to invest in a third. The takeover effectively marked the beginning of the end for Britain's last main line. In the same year, however, brand new DMUs were introduced to operate the service between Derby, Nottingham and Lincoln, the ER having taken control of the route east of Carlton Netherfield from the LMR in 1950. Transferred between regions at the same time was the Southwell branch which did not prosper under its new management. Despite calls to run the new DMU service via the minster town as part of the

Newark-Nottingham timetable, ageing ex-MR locomotives with a single carriage permanently attached continued to operate the intense service of 41 weekday and 43 Saturday trains between Rolleston Junction and Southwell (54) until discontinued in June 1959. Given their success on the Derby-Nottingham-Lincoln route some believed that DMUs could have saved the Southwell passenger service, but elsewhere closure came even where they had been introduced. Less than five months after Southwell lost its passenger trains, the three year old DMU service over the Leverton branch was withdrawn marking the end of travelling by train from the stations of Leverton, Cottam and Torksey (in Lincolnshire).

As passenger services contracted there were more positive achievements with the railways' historic partner the coal industry. In 1952, two years after

54.   The 'Southwell Paddy' – the name given to the Rolleston Junction-Southwell train - photographed from the signalbox at Rolleston Junction on 3rd September 1955. The Nottingham-Lincoln line is in the foreground, with the Southwell branch curving away in the background. *(photo: J. Cupit)*

55. Two locomotives working hard on a Crystal Palace-Sheffield excursion near Hucknall on the former GCR main line on 10th January 1959. Unfortunately, the photographer was not recorded on the print. *(author's collection)*

56. The 16.15 Nottingham Victoria-Pinxton train approaching the former GNR Eastwood & Langley Mill station on 16th August 1958. Another large brick warehouse attests to the importance of goods traffic at almost every station on the rail network before the widespread closures of the 1960s. *(photo: E.C. Haywood)*

57. The former MR station at Mansfield with its generous cast and wrought iron and glass overall roof photographed on 11th April 1951. *(photo: H.B. Priestley/Milepost)*

58. Jubilee class, 4-6-0, no 45650, 'Blake' gets to grips with a Bradford-St Pancras express as it leaves Nottingham and takes the route south-east through West Bridgford, Widmerpool and onto Melton Mowbray in March 1953. Nottingham's St. Mary's church can be seen in the background. *(photo: J.F. Henton)*

59. Stapleford & Sandiacre station photographed on 5th August 1959. The booking office on the road bridge shown here had been provided when the goods lines were extended northwards in 1872, the original 1847 station being taken out of use at that time. *(photo: H.B. Priestley/Milepost)*

the modernisation at Toton, the new pit at Calverton was brought into use with connections to both the former LMS and LNER Leen Valley lines. A new branch incorporating a long concrete viaduct immediately south of the Trent was constructed to connect the new mine at Cotgrave (sunk 1958), to the Nottingham-Grantham line. At the other end of the county, meanwhile, and with a link to the former LD&ECR line east of Ollerton, work had started on Bevercotes Colliery, described at the time as destined to be 'the first fully automated and deepest colliery in the world' although it did not start producing coal until the close of the 1960s.

1962-1973 : The basic railway

The 1960s opened optimistically for freight managers with plans for new coal-fired electricity generating stations about to be realised, all to be fed from Nottinghamshire pits via railway connections. For passenger managers the outlook was bleaker. 'The Reshaping of British Railways' report published at the end of March 1963 was based on straightforward, statistical analysis, with the clear aim of putting the country's railways back into credit by cutting out unprofitable passenger and freight services and as good as relaunching both as new businesses. By then it was painfully obvious that no matter how well many traditional railway services were restructured or promoted they would never cover their operating costs. Change was inevitable.

Although the 'Beeching Plan', as it was nicknamed, was a definite watershed in railway history, the report simply advocated accelerating the relentless process of change that had started before nationalisation. In Nottinghamshire that meant major investment for freight and major surgery for passenger services.

By 1970, as a direct result of 'The Reshaping Report', passenger services had been withdrawn and the routes physically severed between Sheffield, Nottingham Victoria, Leicester Central and London Marylebone (ex-GCR) (55); Nottingham Victoria and Derby Friar Gate (ex-GNR); and Nottingham Victoria and Pinxton (ex-GNR) (56). All stations on the ex-MR Leen Valley line between Nottingham and Shireoaks Junction (for Worksop) had closed (57) with the line under Robin Hood's Hills between Annesley and Kirkby-in-Ashfield taken up and the tunnel filled in. The main line passenger service between Nottingham (MR), Melton Mowbray, Kettering and London, St Pancras (ex-MR) had gone (58), with the line south from Nottingham, over the River Trent and through West Bridgford, taken up. Local stations on the former MR Erewash Valley line (59), including

Trent, and southwards to Leicester (over the ex-MCR main line) had closed although both routes remained vital to freight and main line passenger services. With the closure of Nottingham Victoria in 1967, trains to and from Grantham had been diverted into the ex-MR station for the first time since 1857, using the reinstated junction at Netherfield. The only passenger service targeted for withdrawal in 'The Reshaping Report' but reprieved was that between Nottingham and Lincoln, with all stations (apart from Thorpe-on-the-Hill in Lincolnshire that had closed in 1955) remaining open (60).

Post-Beeching the most important objective for the passenger services that survived was the transportation of people from A to B as economically as possible no matter how meagre the facilities. Some customer service remained at Nottingham, Newark Northgate, Retford and Worksop, but at almost every other station,

60.   A parcels train from Lincoln passing through Newark Castle station on 18th July 1958. This was still a period when British Railways provided decent shelter for passengers waiting for their trains. *(photo: H.B. Priestley/Milepost)*

61. Inside one of the buildings erected by the MR to a standard design to house its steam locomotive fleet at Nottingham. At the time – October 1935 – former London, Tilbury & Southend Railway locomotive, 4-4-2T, no. 2096 was 'on shed'. *(photo: W.Potter)*

booking offices, waiting rooms, toilets and virtually all other platform facilities were withdrawn. The introduction of 'Pay-Trains' (where on-board guards issued the tickets) on all but Nottinghamshire's main lines at the very end of the 1960s saw to this. On the Nottingham-Lincoln and Nottingham-Grantham lines, it was no longer cost-effective to warm up passengers before they got on their trains, nor to feed them or provide facilities for them to relieve themselves. In strict financial terms, it probably had not been so for many years.

Implementation of 'The Reshaping Report' also hastened the end of the steam locomotive. With passenger services cut and the method of handling freight completely overhauled, fewer engines were needed to run the railways. The small ex-MR steam

shed at Southwell had closed in 1955 followed by the former GNR depot at Newark and the old LD&ECR facility at Tuxford in 1959. The former MR shed at Mansfield went out of business the following year and then between 1965 and 1966 the five remaining steam depots in the county were closed: Nottingham (MR) April 1965 (61); Retford (GNR) June 1965; Annesley (GCR) January 1966; Kirkby-in-Ashfield (MR) October 1966; Colwick (GNR) December 1966, (with the whole marshalling yard there closing in April 1970).

Just before the steam Motive Power Depot (MPD) at Toton closed in 1965, a new facility had opened to maintain and service a fleet of diesel locomotives for use all over the East Midlands. By 1971 this new depot had an allocation of 356 diesels of which 25 spent all their working days shunting in and around the complex. Twenty-five years earlier, on the eve of nationalisation, the total number of steam locomotives allocated to depots just in Nottinghamshire had been just over twice that number.

After Beeching's surgery there was a debilitating calm. The railways were somewhat punch drunk; if they had been hit again they would not have felt any pain. For the next few years they ran mechanically, apparently without enthusiasm, certainly without vision, keeping a low profile as if to avoid criticism and possible further cuts. All services were modular and bland like the blue and white corporate livery of the trains that operated them. All trains between Nottingham and Lincoln stopped at all stations, started no further a field than Derby and went no further than Lincolnshire's county town. If you wanted to travel further, you changed trains somewhere: Nottingham to Birmingham meant a change at Derby; Nottingham to Mansfield meant a trip by bus, car or taxi. It would take a new generation of politicians to rediscover the word 'potential' in relation to railways.

The only significant investment immediately post-Beeching was in freight services. Although a completely discredited aim at the time of writing (2010), the extraction, transport and burning of coal to generate electricity, was the major area of investment. As the steam locomotive was banished from the rail network and thousands of homes turned their backs on open coal fires, electricity from the county's new breed of power stations stretched out along the Trent heralded a cleaner and healthier society. At the time, it was hailed as one of the big success stories of the country's nationalised railway, coal mining and electricity industries, a success story centred on Nottinghamshire and Yorkshire.

The first of the new generation rail connected, electricity power stations was High Marnham

brought on stream in 1959 and fed from the west off the former LD&ECR line. This was followed by Staythorpe B opened in 1962 next to the existing 1950 power station receiving coal trains off the Nottingham-Lincoln line. The next two plants - West Burton (1967) and Cottam (1968) – precipitated a major piece of civil engineering work at Retford to cope with the new flow of coal trains to and from those sites. Completed in 1965 it involved diverting the Shireoaks-Worksop-Retford line under the East Coast main line where since 1852 the two routes had intersected on the level (62). The former GCR steam shed was swept away as part of the work and, for the first time since 1859, platforms reappeared on the old MS&LR line at Retford. The moth-balled Leverton branch west of the Trent was also brought back into use with new signalling to give Cottam access to the rail network. The way coal was delivered to both West Burton and Cottam power stations fulfilled one of the ideals championed in 'The Reshaping Report' – the use of new 32ton capacity wagons worked in fixed 'Merry-go-round' (MGR) trains and operated (theoretically), as the title implied, non-stop between loading and delivery (63).

The last of the new generation of power stations to reach full capacity was Ratcliffe-on-Soar in 1969. It too had been designed to be fed by MGR trains and although the ideal of continuous operation was never fully achieved, by the 1980s MGR trains were the most efficiently run of any freight service in terms of manning and the utilisation of locomotives and wagons. Before the contraction of the mining industry in that decade, Ratcliffe power station consumed 65% of the total output of south Nottinghamshire pits, just over 14m tonnes a year, all coming in by rail. At the time this was considered an accolade but may now be viewed as more of an environmental catastrophe.

1973-1993 : Parkway to Privatisation

Despite the Labour Party's victory in the General Election of 1964 there was no attempt to halt the

62. The north-bound 'Flying Scotsman' hauled by a 'Deltic' diesel locomotive crosses the former MS&LR/GCR line at Retford on 5th March 1963. *(photo: British Railways, ER)*

63. On 4th May 1979 a train of empty coal wagons travelling north bound for Annesley, passes the site of Hucknall's MR station. To the right, a 'Merry-go-round' train is passing under the huge concrete loading bunker of Hucknall Colliery (No.2). The colliery closed in October 1986 seven years after this photograph was taken; seven years after that a new passenger station was built here, opening in May 1993. *(photo:A.R. Kaye)*

implementation of 'The Reshaping Report'. Instead a working party was set up to look at ways of balancing commercialism and running costs with social need. The idea of the social railway was born and with it British Railways' annual struggle for subsidies. The first grant-aid list was published in November 1968 and between then and 1973 (when the way subsidies were allocated was revised), approaching £3m was paid in grant-aid for services between Nottingham & Lincoln, Nottingham & Grantham, Sheffield & Lincoln (via Retford), and Nottingham & Derby. Inflation in this period was severe. The Nottingham-Lincoln service received £188,000 in the first year compared with £239,000 in 1973.

But as British Rail and the Government argued over subsidies, there were signs of a more positive approach to railway matters. By the beginning of the 1970s, Mansfield's isolation from the railway network was the subject of definite plans to rectify the problem, and largely disinterested since the 1920s, local authorities once again became actively involved in railway issues. Planning authorities in both Nottinghamshire and Derbyshire were discussing how best to give Mansfield and its neighbours better access to rail services. In the summer of 1970 the idea of reinstating a passenger service over the former MR's Leen Valley line was rejected, and attention turned instead to the reopening of Alfreton station (in Derbyshire) on the former MR Erewash Valley line where main-line, inter-city trains could be timetabled to stop. In 1972 plans were agreed with British Rail and with a contribution from eleven local authorities either side of the border to the costs of providing buildings, a carpark and bus connections, Alfreton & Mansfield Parkway station

64. A reminder of when holidays started with soot and smoke before sun and sea could be reached. The Holiday Express at Nottingham (MR) station sometime in the 1950s. *(author's collection)*

65. South-bound HST photographed at Muskham just after midday on 3rd January 1991 passing the site where the Great North Road (A1) crossed the GNR main line between the two cottages until 1929 when Nottinghamshire County Council paid for a bridge to be built. *(photo: author)*

opened on 7th May the following year. The initiative was hailed as a success at the time and interestingly one of the reasons given was its use for seasonal holiday traffic. This ran completely contrary to the Beeching philosophy of concentrating only on regular traffic flows whilst eliminating routes and stations such as Mablethorpe and Skegness that were perceived as cost-effective for only a few months a year (64). (Both Mablethorpe and Skegness had been on Beeching's closure list, only the latter retaining its link with the railway network).

The next positive milestone for the railways of Nottinghamshire (as elsewhere in the country) was the dividing up of British Rail into business 'sectors' in 1982. This was a form of internal privatisation and it really marks the start of the kind of railway services we are familiar with today (2010). The work of these sectors made the Conservative

Party's privatisation of British Rail in 1994 both possible and attractive to private companies (bolstered by some generous pump-priming subsidies). In the 1982 reorganisation, express passenger services became the responsibility of 'Inter-City' with local services, such as those between Nottingham, Grantham and Lincoln and through Worksop administered by the, depressingly christened, 'Provincial' sector (renamed 'Regional Railways' in 1990). Freight traffic was also divided up into new sectors.

Both passenger sectors benefited enormously from the introduction of new trains, High Speed Trains (HSTs) on Inter-City routes and a new generation of DMUs christened 'Sprinters' for other services. HSTs had started running on the East Coast main line through Retford and Newark in 1978 and despite the recession of the early 1980s, the increased frequency and reduced journey times

66. One of the first generation of 'Sprinters' leaving Lowdham station on 28th August 1986 with a service to Newark and Lincoln. *(photo: author)*

67. A view from Lincoln Road bridge looking south as a new electric service heading for London, Kings Cross (moving away from the camera) enters Newark Northgate station on a summer evening in 1992. The redundant goods yard on the right sensibly became an extension to the station carpark a few years later. *(photo: author)*

they offered boosted passenger numbers (65). For a time, Newark was being billed as a commuter town for London! Less dramatic claims were made when HSTs were introduced on Nottingham-London, St Pancras services at the end of 1982, but over and above the faster journey times they offered, HSTs undoubtedly helped change British Rail's image for the better.

The 'Provincial' sector was not so swift at improving its services. In Nottinghamshire the first new 'Sprinters' were put into service in 1986 (66), but it was not until later models began to appear at the beginning of the 1990s, replacing the last of the 1950s DMUs, that noticeable improvements were possible. The very latest units were not only capable of fast acceleration but express passenger speeds – something which a decade earlier would have been considered only possible by locomotive-hauled trains. The full benefits for passengers did not materialise until after privatisation, but there is no doubt that the revolution began under Regional Railways' management.

One of the very last achievements of British Rail also produced enormous benefits for Nottinghamshire travellers. This was the electrification of the East Coast main line between London, Kings Cross and Edinburgh. Ironically it was not to be the first line passing through Nottinghamshire to be equipped for electric trains. That accolade goes to a stretch of the former MR main line between just south of Edwalton station and Old Dalby in Leicestershire that had closed in 1968 and had been taken over by British Rail's Research Department based in Derby. The route was partly fitted with overhead cables so that the electric version of the Advanced Passenger Train (APT) could be tested there in 1970-73. A more dramatic use of the line occurred in July 1984 when a diesel locomotive was crashed into an empty Nuclear Flask wagon to test its resistance to an 80 mph impact. The staged accident actually took place over the border in Leicestershire,

although the engine had started its fatal run in Nottinghamshire!

Electrification of the East Coast main line had been proposed in the 1955 Modernisation Plan and again in 1973, the latter proposals also including a promise to electrify the route between London, St Pancras and Leeds embracing both Nottingham and Derby. Funds were not forth-coming in either year and it was not until July 1984 that the government was finally persuaded to fund the East Coast work. It was a huge undertaking although rationalisation and resignalling in the 1970s had helped to pave the way. A full electric service between Kings Cross and Edinburgh, through Newark (67) and Retford started in the summer of 1991 and the reduction in journey times and the increased frequency of trains is well illustrated in Table 2.

* not 1956 as stated in the author's 'Rail Centres: Nottingham', (p.96).

Chapter 7

Privatisation

Although actually completed after privatisation arguably, the best achievement of British Rail in Nottinghamshire (although some might say it merely righted a wrong inflicted by the same organisation twenty years earlier) was the re-establishment of a direct railway link between Nottingham and Worksop utilising most of the former MR Leen Valley line. With the relentless closure of collieries in Nottinghamshire (29 between 1980 and 2009) the local authorities viewed the reinstatement of the passenger service as an integral part of their plans to stimulate alternative employment opportunities and improve access to the city for former mining communities. Some sources claim that between 1983 and 1995, 32,500 mining jobs were lost in Nottinghamshire.

The 'Robin Hood Line' project was launched in the mid-1980s and eventually saw the opening of new stations at Bulwell, Hucknall, Newstead, Kirkby-in-Ashfield, Sutton Parkway, Mansfield, Mansfield Woodhouse, Shirebrook, Langwith & Whaley Thorns, Creswell and Whitwell (the last three being in Derbyshire). A service between Nottingham, Hucknall and Newstead was reintroduced in May 1993 with Bulwell station opening in 1994. By then work had started on Phase Two northwards from Newstead. As the track between Annesley and Kirkby-in-Ashfield on this part of the ex-MR had been lifted in 1970, the embankment north of Annesley being removed and Kirkby Tunnel and its approach cuttings filled in, this stage was the most costly of the whole project. It was officially costed at £21m.

There had been fears the tunnel might have suffered from colliery subsidence but, fortunately, this was not the case. North of Kirkby Tunnel engineers deviated from the original MR route laying tracks along the former GCR main line to the site of Kirkby South Junction where the ex-GNR Leen Valley Extension line of 1897-1900 had

branched off. The rock cuttings here had also been filled with domestic waste since closure but as the exit from Kirkby Tunnel put the new line higher than both the GCR and GNR routes, the waste could be left in-situ and tracks laid on top. A new junction was then created to link up with the existing line through Kirkby-in-Ashfield that had remained open for colliery traffic, part of the ex-MR route between its Erewash Valley line at Pye Bridge and the former MS&LR/GCR line at Shireoaks. The surviving line through Kirkby-in-Ashfield, however, was not on the alignment of the original MR Leen Valley route but on that of the former GNR Leen Valley Extension. Because the MR route in the town had two level crossings, it was abandoned in 1972 in favour of the GNR route which caused no road traffic disruption. And it was this decision that led to one of those little ironies of railway history. As detailed in previous chapters, both the GCR and MR had stations serving Kirkby-in-Ashfield (closed in 1956 and 1964 respectively), but the GNR, even though its Leen Valley Extension line ran very close by and between its two rivals, never provided a station for the community. However, as this company's route was the only one remaining in the town it was on the former GNR line that the new 'Robin Hood Line' station for Kirkby-in-Ashfield was opened in November 1996 (68). The station was an afterthought as what has become Sutton Parkway (built on the original MR Leen Valley line half a mile south of its first station and close to the site of Summit Colliery), had been planned to serve both Kirkby and Sutton-in-Ashfield and opened a year earlier in November 1995. That month also marked the triumphant return of Mansfield and Mansfield Woodhouse to the railway map, the 1973 Alfreton & Mansfield Parkway station being renamed simply Alfreton at the same time. The surviving ex-MR goods shed at Mansfield Woodhouse became the temporary terminal station until the extension to Shireoaks was completed and it was not too long before the MR's station building at Mansfield was back in railway use after being purchased by the District Council.

68. The 9.49 departure for Nottingham waits at Kirkby-in-Ashfield station on 10th March 2010. *(photo: author)*

69. A GNER HST in its smart deep blue and red livery approaches Newark Crossing with a service for London, Kings Cross on 4th June 2000. Running across the photograph from left to right is the MR's 1846 Nottingham-Lincoln line. In the background the train has just passed through the 1889 steel bridge across the Trent Navigation, (the adjacent bridge span was finished the following year). Next to both Victorian bridges is the 21st century replacement waiting to be pushed into place during the night of 26th/27th August 2000. *(photo: author)*

Completion of the route through to Worksop via Shireoaks Junction was finally achieved in spring 1998, a special VIP train being run on 11th May followed by a full public service from 25th of that month. The whole 'Robin Hood Line' project has been a very impressive achievement for all the local authorities, civil engineers and train operators involved.

It is claimed by some that projects like the 'Robin Hood Line' are now far more difficult to achieve following privatisation of the railways. What privatisation did, which had never been done before, was to separate all the functions of the industry and to offer them as a fixed-term franchise to any business which could prove it could do the work. Subsidies were offered in return for achieving targets. So for the first time in railway history, the company maintaining the track was completely independent of the business that ran the trains – which, in turn, was independent of the business that supplied them. The new train operating companies inherited services that had improved noticeably since British Rail had been divided into sectors in 1982 and they continued the improvements benefiting (as indeed would a nationalised railway system) from the introduction of new trains.

It was these new trains, coupled with a congested road system, that did much to encourage people back to the railways. Passenger numbers began to increase. As more cross-country trains were added to the timetable (see Table 2), platform 6 at Nottingham station was reopened in 1999. Privatisation got the credit for the renaissance but in the case of the East Coast main line through Newark and Retford, it would have taken an extremely incompetent operator not to have made a success of running a passenger service on a newly electrified route with a fleet of brand new, state of the art, trains. The franchise awarded to Sea Containers in April 1996 was branded Great North Eastern Railway (GNER) and so successful was this business that by the beginning of the 21st

Century it had plans for the introduction of tilting trains running at 140mph. Matching Sea Containers' optimism was that of Railtrack (the rump of British Rail formed in 1994 but not privatised until 1996, tasked with maintaining the rail network), confidently promising a raft of track improvements including the removal of the flat crossing at Newark (69). This crossing, where the Nottingham-Lincoln line crosses the East Coast main line on the level, was planned to be replaced by a bridge to be completed by 2007. Such plans, however, came before the disastrous Hatfield accident of October 2000 after which all the hype of privatisation was suddenly seen in a completely different light and priorities changed dramatically. Tilting trains have not materialised, the Newark flat crossing remains stubbornly in place and, at the time of writing (2010), both the former GNER passenger services and the former Railtrack responsibilities are back in Government (public) hands – the return of a little bit of British Rail.

There is no doubt that, at its height, GNER had been a success story. An even more dramatic change, however, was to benefit travellers between Nottingham and London in the first decade of the 21st century. In the space of less than five years, the number of trains running between those two places almost doubled. When Midland Mainline won the franchise to run the service on this route in the 1990s, it inherited HST's from British Rail but it was not too long before it optimistically decided to order a fleet of new trains that were eventually christened 'Meridians' (70). The first came into use in June 2004 and by the time the franchise had passed to East Midlands Trains in November 2007, the transformation of the Nottingham-St Pancras service was complete. From 19 weekday trains between Nottingham and London in 2003, the current 2010 timetable advertises 32, with 33 northbound in place of just 16. One can only speculate as to whether or not the same investment in the service would have been made under British Rail, Inter-City management.

Privatisation certainly injected a spirit of enterprise back into various parts of the rail industry but partly because this resulted in the fragmentation of the railway's functions, what has yet to be delivered is the opening of new stations. In the first couple of years of the 1990s, British Rail's Regional Railways sector, working closely with local authorities, had confidently expected to reopen stations at Ilkeston, Trowell, Sandiacre, Long Eaton (Central), Lenton and Gedling with new ones planned for Wollaton, Cotgrave, Saxondale (Park & Ride) and Ratcliffe (Park & Ride). Only the latter has appeared as East Midlands Parkway, opened by local MP and former Transport Minister, Geoff Hoon, on 26th January 2009, six years later than planned.

Heritage losses post 1963

Only a tiny proportion of all the steam locomotives, diesels, carriages and wagons used in Nottinghamshire since 1839 have survived. That is to be expected. By comparison, there is much left of the railway's infrastructure – buildings, bridges, tunnels (71), etc. most of it Victorian. Throughout the 19th century and up to the start of the First World War, the private railway companies were continually adding to their portfolio of buildings and until the 1960s almost all this legacy remained intact.

As we have seen, the period of management by British Railways witnessed massive changes in services but, unlike preceding decades, it was also a period that saw the loss of many more railway

70. A London, St Pancras-Nottingham 'Meridian' service (moving away from the camera) slowing for its stop at East Midlands Parkway on 7th March 2010, Ratcliffe-on-Soar power station in the background. *(photo: author)*

71. Watnall Tunnel on the GNR's 1875 Derbyshire & Staffordshire Extension line; 13th August 1965. To the east of the tunnel a 2.5 mile cutting had to be excavated through solid rock. So time consuming was the work, and so anxious was the GNR to get coal moving from the Erewash Valley, that a temporary line was laid over the top of the tunnel. Less than a hundred years later the cutting and tunnel became a land-fill site for building waste. *(photo: J. Marshall/Kidderminster Railway Museum)*

buildings and structures than ever before. For many reasons it is obvious that trains have a limited life in service, but the infrastructure is capable of continual maintenance and adaptation to changing needs if the desire is there. Until the 1960s, Victorian structures were kept in use mainly because they were still serving the purpose for which they had been built. They were not maintained for their architectural or heritage merits. Once their original purpose had ceased, the only response in the 1960s was to demolish. British Rail only adapted buildings when it was considered too costly to demolish and replace, and very few were sold to be adapted for non-railway purposes. At Newark Northgate station, for example, adaptation of all the 1880s brick buildings with canopies supported by decorative cast-iron on the London-bound (up) platform to cater for passengers using the diverted London to

Cleethorpes service was a possibility but obviously a compelling financial case was made to demolish them all in 1973 and erect pre-fabricated wooden cabins in their place.

At Retford there was a more convincing argument for demolition of ex-GNR buildings and canopies on the north-bound (down) platform because the track needed to be realigned to allow faster passing speeds. The skyline west of Nottingham Midland station, meanwhile, changed dramatically in the 1990s with the demolition of the all but one of the former MR goods, grain and bonded warehouses (8). The distribution of goods gave way to the distribution of justice with the erection of the new Magistrates' Courts and Bridewell, and where once the Potato Warehouse stood, a new county archives office appeared.

72. Another piece of GNR civil engineering photographed on 13th December 1958. Giltbrook Viaduct, between Kimberley and Awsworth, described a slight 'S' shape as it crossed the valley. It was 523m (1716ft) long, 18.2m (60ft) at its highest point, and gave the GNR access into the Erewash coalfield in 1875. A four storey set of cottages with a total of eight rooms, all with windows and fireplaces, was built into one of the arches. This impressive structure went out of railway use in 1964, was considered for preservation, but demolished in 1973. *(photo: E.C. Haywood)*

73. The ex-LD&ECR Fledborough viaduct, only part of which is showing in this photograph taken on 27th November 2009 looking north along the River Trent. The white trails in the background are emanating from Cottam power station. *(photo: author)*

Probably only railway enthusiasts regret the loss of bridges, viaducts and tunnels, but it is certainly a fact that during the last three decades most of the former GNR and GCR's presence in the Erewash and Leen valleys and around Nottingham has been eradicated with the removal or infilling, of miles of substantial and well-built brick structures (72). It would be tedious to name them all but the differing fates of three are worth mentioning here. The GCR's generous six steel spans across the River Trent south of Nottingham came down with their blue brick approach arches in 1985, no use being found for a river crossing at this point. By comparison the MR's bridge across the Trent that had put Nottingham on a through north-south, main line route for the first time in 1879, was considered suitable for conversion into a road bridge exactly one hundred years later in 1979. A structure that might have been repaired for continued railway use was the GCR's viaduct through Broad Marsh. But it was not to be, and in 2003 having stood defiantly since the last train used it in 1974, it was demolished, replaced by a new concrete viaduct of almost the same dimensions on exactly the same alignment built to support the tracks of part of the Nottingham Express Transit (NET) system opened at the beginning of March 2004 between the railway station and Hucknall via the city centre.

The listing of buildings has helped prolong the life of a select few railway structures: Nottingham Midland, Beeston, Newark Castle, and Worksop station buildings still used for railway purposes are listed Grade II along with two former MR viaducts in Mansfield and the two northern portals of Redhill tunnels. The 1857 Nottingham terminus of the Ambergate, Nottingham & Boston & Eastern Junction Railway (London Road Low Level) and Thurgarton station buildings both abandoned by British Rail are also listed Grade II. Others structures no longer in railway use, but not always listed, have been refurbished and put to new uses. The clock tower of Nottingham Victoria Station stands as a forlorn monument, but the ex-MR goods warehouse at Newark was converted into flats in the 1990s.

But not all ex-railway buildings that find new uses are guaranteed a long retirement; Nottingham's London Road High Level station, closed in 1967, was finally demolished in 2006 after a precarious life as an antique centre, office furniture supplier and restaurant. Unknown to all but a few railway enthusiasts, local farmers and anglers, the LD&ECR's impressive viaduct over the Trent at Fledborough (73) still survives but with no further use, for how much longer?

Gone too are large tracts of railway land once occupied by extensive sidings. Sensibly at places such as Newark Northgate, former goods yards have become station carparks, but elsewhere all manner of non-railway industrial units, trading estates, leisure facilities and offices have ensured the railway will never reoccupy lineside locations again. As this condensed history was being written, a brand new, architecturally provocative building to house contemporary art was opened in Nottingham, plugging the south end of the GCR's Thurland Street tunnel at Weekday Cross and finally putting an end to any hope for a transport corridor between Broad Marsh and Victoria Shopping Centre.

Bibliography

A-Z of Rail Reopenings,
Railway Development Society, 1998
(with 1999 supplement)

Aldworth, C.,
The Nottingham & Melton Railway 1872-1990,
Colin Aldworth, 1990

Anderson, P.H.,
Forgotten Railways: vol.2 The East Midlands,
David & Charles, 1973, 1985

Birch, D.G.,
The story of the Nottingham Suburban Railway,
Book Law, 2010

Bradshaw's April 1910 Railway Guide,
David & Charles, 1968

Bradshaw's July 1922 Railway Guide,
David & Charles, 1985

Bradshaw's July 1938 Railway Guide,
David & Charles, 1969

Bradshaw's British Railways Guide,
6.10.1947-31.10.1947

Bradshaw's British Railways Guide,
21.9.1953-31.10.1953

British Railway Passenger Services Timetable,
LMR, 9.9.1963-14.6.1964

British Railway Passenger Services Timetable,
ER, 9.9.1963-14.6.1964

British Rail Passenger Timetable,
LMR, 1.5.1972-6.5.1973

British Rail Passenger Timetable,
16.5.1983-13.5.1984

British Rail Passenger Timetable,
17.5.1993-3.10.1993

British Railways Pre-Grouping Atlas & Gazetteer,
fifth edition, Ian Allan, 1976

Butt, R.V.J.,
The Directory of Railway Stations,
Patrick Stephens, 1995

Clinker, C.R.,
Clinker's Register of Closed Passenger Stations & Goods Depots, 1830-1977,
Avon Anglia, 1978

Daniels, G. & Dench. L.,
Passengers No More,
Ian Allan, (?1963)

Derby Railway History Research Group,
The Midland Counties Railway,
Railway & Canal Historical Society, 1989

Dow, G.,
Great Central,
vols. 1-2, Locomotive Publishing Co.,1959, 1962,
vol. 3, Ian Allan, 1965

Forster, V. & Taylor, W.,
Scenes from the Past: Railways in and Around Nottingham,
Foxline, 1991

Goode, C.T.,
The Railways of Nottingham,
1991

Goode, C.T.,
Railway Rambles on the Notts & Derbyshire Border,
1983

Gough, J.,
The Midland Railway, a chronology,
Railway & Canal Historical Society, 1989

Gough, J.,
British Rail at Work; the East Midlands,
Ian Allan, 1985

Grinling, C.H.,
The History of the Great Northern Railway
(with additional chapters by H.V. Borley &
C.Hamilton Ellis), Allen & Unwin 1966
(first published 1898)

Henshaw, A.,
The Great Northern Railway in the East Midlands,
vols. 1-3, Railway Travel & Correspondence
Society, 1999, 2000

Hurst, G.,
The Midland Railway around Nottinghamshire,
Milepost, 1987

Hurst, G.,
Great Central East of Sheffield,
Milepost, 1989

Leleux, R.,
*Volume 9, The East Midlands; Regional History of
the Railways of Great Britain*,
David & Charles, 1976

Midland Railway System Maps,
vol. 2, Peter Kay, 199?

Munns, R.T.,
*Milk Churns to Merry-go-Round; a century of train
operation*,
David & Charles, 1986

National Rail Timetable,
18.5.2003-27.9.2003

Nock, O.S.,
The Great Northern Railway,
Ian Allan, 1958

Perkins, C.J. & Padgett. R.,
The Midland Railway in Nottingham;
vol.1 1839-1907, C.J. Perkins, 2000

*Railway Clearing House Official Hand Book of
Railway Stations, 1904*,
David & Charles, 1970

*Railway Clearing House Official Hand Book of
Railway Stations, 1925*

Railway Correspondence & Travel Society
(East Midlands Branch),
The Railways of Nottingham,
(exhibition catalogue), 1969

Reed, H.J.,
The Rise & Fall of Nottingham's Railway Network,
vols. 1 & 2, Book Law, 2007

Robotham, R.,
Great Central Railway's London Extension,
Ian Allan, 1999

*Timetables of the Midland Railway, July, August &
September 1903*,
Ian Allan, (reprint nd)

Vanns, M.A.,
Rail Centres: Nottingham,
Ian Allan, 1993

Vanns, M.A.,
The Railways of Newark-on-Trent,
Oakwood Press, 1999

Waite, P.B.,
*Railways of Nottingham, History of the Great
Northern Colwick Motive Power Depot and
Marshalling Yard*,
Book Law, 2004

Williams, F.S.,
The Midland Railway its Rise & Progress,
fifth edition, F.S. Williams, 1886

Wilson, J.P.,
The Development of Nottingham's Railways,
Nottingham Civic Society, (1969nd)

Wrottesley, J.,
The Great Northern Railway,
vols. 1-3, Batsford, 1979, 1981

Table 1

This table compares the times of a selection of through trains exactly one hundred years apart, in 1910 and 2010, the date this book was published.

through weekday trains only	1910 no.	1910 fastest	1910 notes	2010 no.	2010 fastest	2010 notes
Nottingham MR - London, St Pancras	7	2hr 15min	MR trains	32	1hr 43min	
Nottingham Victoria (GN&GCJ) - London, Kings Cross	2	2hr 25min (Luncheon Car Express, 11.00-13.25)	GNR trains		no through trains	
Nottingham Victoria (GN&GCJ) - London, Marylebone	9	2hr 23min	GCR trains		route no longer available	
London, St Pancras - Nottingham MR	9	2hr 15min	MR trains	33	1hr 44min	
London, Kings Cross - Nottingham Victoria (GN&GCJ)	1	2hr 36min (Dining Car Express to York & Newcastle, 17.30-20.06)	GNR train		no through trains	
London, Marylebone - Nottingham Victoria (GN&GCJ)	7	2hr 21min	GCR trains		route no longer available	
Retford - London, Kings Cross	10	2hr 33min	GNR trains	11	1hr 29min	
London, Kings Cross - Retford	13	2hr 48min	GNR trains	12	1hr 18min	
Newark GN - London, Kings Cross	10	2hr 31min	GNR trains	29	1hr 17min	renamed Newark Northgate after 1950
London, Kings Cross - Newark GN	8	2hr 31min	GNR trains	29	1hr 16min	
Nottingham Victoria (GN&GCJ) - Manchester (London Road)	9	2hr	GCR trains	15	1hr 52min	Nottingham (MR) - Manchester Piccadilly (renamed from London Road after 1960)
Manchester (London Road) - Nottingham Victoria (GN&GCJ)	9	2hr 2min	GCR trains	15	1hr 47min	Manchester Piccadilly - Nottingham (MR)
Nottingham MR - Norwich	1	3hr 35min (15.10-18.45)	M&GNJR train to and from Norwich City (closed 1959)	14	2hr 38min	Norwich Thorpe
Norwich - Nottingham MR	1	3hr 35min (9.50-13.25)	M&GNJR train to and from Norwich City (closed 1959)	14	2hr 38min	Norwich Thorpe
Nottingham MR - Birmingham New Street		no through trains	journey achieved by changing trains at Derby	30	1hr 13min	
Birmingham New Street - Nottingham MR		no through trains	journey achieved by changing trains at Derby	31	1hr 9min	
Nottingham Victoria (GN&GCJ) - Skegness	(2)	1, MO & ThO 1hr 55min (8.45-10.40) 1, FO & SO 1hr 57min (17.40-19.37)	GNR trains	14	1hr 55min	Nottingham (MR) - Skegness
Skegness - Nottingham Victoria (GN&GCJR)	(2)	1, MO 1hr 55min (7.40-9.35) 1, MO & ThO 2hr 2min (18.15-20.17)		15	1hr 52min	Skegness - Nottingham (MR)
Worksop - Lincoln Central	10	41min	GCR trains via Leverton Branch	16	52min	via Gainsborough
Lincoln Central - Worksop	9	39min	GCR trains via Leverton Branch	15	47min	via Gainsborough
Worksop - Manchester (London Road)	6	1hr 44min	GCR trains via Leverton Branch		no through trains	
Manchester (London Road) - Worksop	6	1hr 45min	GCR trains via Leverton Branch		no through trains	
Nottingham MR – Derby MR	30	23min	MR trains	51	20min	
Nottingham Victoria (GN&GCJ) - Derby Friargate	17	29min	GNR trains		route no longer available	
Derby MR - Nottingham MR	33	30min	MR trains	50	24min	
Derby Friargate - Nottingham Victoria (GN&GCJ)	18	31min	GNR trains		route no longer available	

Table 2

This table compares the times of a selection of through trains in ten year intervals starting in 1963, the year of the publication of 'The Reshaping Report' (the 'Beeching Plan'); 1973 when there were no more regular steam trains; 1983 a year after British Rail was divided into 'sectors' and High Speed Trains had been introduced on most services between Retford, Newark Northgate and London, Kings Cross, and Nottingham (MR) and St Pancras; 1993 the last year of a fully nationalised railway network managed by British Rail; 2003 ten years after the passing of the Railway Privatisation Act.

through weekday trains only	1963 no.	fastest	1973 no.	fastest	1983 no.	fastest	1993 no.	fastest	2003 no.	fastest
Nottingham (MR) - London, St Pancras	13	1hr 56min (Midland Pullman, first class only) 2hr (all classes)	16	1hr 57min	15	1hr 39min	15	1hr 33min The Robin Hood Pullman	19	1hr 40min
London, St Pancras - Nottingham (MR)	13	1hr 55min (Midland Pullman, first class only) 2hr (all classes)	17	1hr 55min	16	1hr 39min	17	1hr 37min	16	1hr 39min
Retford -London, Kings Cross	3	2hr 24min	13	1hr 59min (Hull Pullman)	14	1hr 29min	11	1hr 35min	12	1hr 32min
London, Kings Cross - Retford	5	2hr 32min	10	1hr 56min (Hull Pullman)	12	1hr 28min	10	1hr 31min	12	1hr 18min
Newark, Northgate - London, Kings Cross	2	2hr 14min	15	1hr 50min	18	1hr 16min	19	1hr 24min	23	1hr 18min
London, Kings Cross - Newark, Northgate	4	2hr 12min	12	1hr 49min	15	1hr 13min	21	1hr 14min	25	1hr 11min
Nottingham (MR) - Manchester (* Manchester Victoria) (** Manchester Piccadilly)		no through trains (1, MX, Nottingham Victoria - Manchester Piccadilly, 2hr 34min)		no through trains	3	2hr 24min*	15	1hr 47min**	15	1hr 54min**
Manchester - Nottingham (MR)		no through trains (1, MX, Manchester Piccadilly - Nottingham Victoria, 2hr 50min)		no through trains	3	2hr 18min*	15	1hr 42min**	16	1hr 42min**
Nottingham (MR) - Norwich		no through trains		no through trains		no through trains	6	2hr 30min	14	2hr 34min
Norwich - Nottingham (MR)		no through trains		no through trains		no through trains	6	2hr 43min	12	2hr 28min
Nottingham (MR) - Birmingham New Street		no through trains	2	1hr 51min	7	1hr 30min	16	1hr 13min	37	1hr 16min
Birmingham New Street - Nottingham (MR)		no through trains	1	2hr 3min	1	1hr 36min (16.09-17.45)	16	1hr 9min	33	1hr 7min
Nottingham (MR) - Skegness		no through trains (except summer excursions)	3	2hr 22min	5	1hr 54min (school holidays except Fridays & Saturdays)	11	1hr 57min (school holidays only)	14	1hr 44min
Skegness - Nottingham (MR)		no through trains (except summer excursions)		no through trains except 3, SO	4	2hr 29min	12	1hr 45min (school holidays only)	14	1hr 40min
Worksop - Lincoln Central	8	50min	11	51min	9	48min	9	48min	15	51min
Lincoln Central - Worksop	6	49min	9	50min	10	51min	9	46min	15	48min
Worksop - Manchester Piccadilly	1	1hr 26min	3	1hr 42min		no through trains		no through trains		no through trains
Manchester Piccadilly - Worksop	2	1hr 19min	3	1hr 40min	1	1hr 38min		no through trains		no through trains

Table 3

Nottinghamshire stations in alphabetical order using the last or latest official name; opening and closing dates (passenger services listed first)

NAME (current or at closure to passengers)	ORIGINAL COMPANY	DATE OPENED	DATE CLOSED	NOTES
Annesley	MR	1.7.1874	6.4.1953 (passengers and goods)	
Arkwright Street	GCR	15.3.1899; 4.9.1967	4.3.1963; 5.5.1969	no facilities for goods
Aslockton	ANBEJR	15.7.1850	15.6.1964 (goods)	still open for passengers (2010)
Attenborough Gate	MR	1.12.1856	1.11.1858	temporary 'request stop'
Attenborough	MR	1.9.1864?	-	permanent station adjacent to 'Attenborough Gate' level crossing; no facilities for goods; still open for passengers (2010)
Awsworth	GNR	1.11.1880	7.9.1964 (passengers); 1.6.1943 (goods)	
Barnby Moor & Sutton	GNR	4.9.1849	7.11.1949	originally named 'Sutton' until 16.11.1909; no facilities for goods
Barnstone	GN&LNWJR	1.9.1879	7.12.1953 (passengers); 10.9.1962 (goods)	spelling altered to 'Barnston' between 11.1889 & 1.8.1897
Basford Vernon	MR	1.12.1848?	4.1.1960 (passengers); 2.10.1967 (goods)	originally named 'Basford' until 1.7.1950 (goods) and 11.8.1952 (passengers)
Basford North	GNR	1.2.1876	7.9.1964 (passengers); 2.10.1967 (goods)	originally due to be named Dob Park but opened as 'New Basford & Bulwell'; renamed 'Basford & Bulwell' 1.8.1876; renamed 'Basford North' 1.7.1950 (goods), 21.9.1953 (passengers)
Beckingham	GNR	15.7.1867 (passengers); 1.7.1867 (goods)	2.11.1959 (passengers); 19.8.1963 (goods)	
Beeston	MCR	4.6.1839	29.12.1969 (goods)	still open for passengers (2010)
Bestwood Colliery	GNR	2.10.1882	14.9.1931 (passengers); 7.4.1958 (goods)	originally named 'Bestwood' until 3.1883
Bingham	ANBEJR	15.7.1850	2.8.1965 (goods)	still open for passengers (2010)
Bingham Road	GN&LNWJR	1.9.1879	2.7.1951	no facilities for goods
Bleasby	MR	1.10.1850		originally a 'request stop' adjacent to the level crossing at 'Bleasby Gate' from 1848; no facilities for goods; still open for passengers (2010)
Blidworth & Rainworth	MR	3.4.1871	12.8.1929 (passengers); 1.2.1965 (goods)	originally named 'Rainworth'; renamed 'Blidworth' 1.5.1877; renamed 'Blidworth & Rainworth' 27.4.1894; a replacement bus service was laid on by the LMS when the station closed to passengers
Boughton	LD&ECR	15.12.1896	19.9.1955 (passengers); 4.1.1965 (goods)	
Bulwell Market	MR	2.10.1848	12.10.1964 (passengers); 7.8.1967 (goods)	originally named 'Bulwell' until 1.7.1950 (goods) and 11.8.1952 (passengers)
Bulwell	BR/RT	27.5.1994	-	no facilities for goods; still open for passengers (2010)
Bulwell Common	GCR	15.3.1899 (passengers); 11.4.1899 (goods)	4.3.1963	
Bulwell Forest	GNR	1.10.1887	23.9.1929 (passengers); 7.4.1958 (goods)	
Bulwell Hall Halt	GCR	24.4.1909	5.5.1930	no facilities for goods
Burton Joyce	MR	4.8.1846 (passengers); 1.5.1889 (goods)	27.4.1964 (goods)	still open for passengers (2010)
Butler's Hill	GNR	2.10.1882	14.9.1931 (passengers); 26.9.1932 (parcels)	
Carlton	MR	4.8.1846	2.8.1965 (goods)	originally named 'Carlton' until 1.11.1871 when it was renamed 'Carlton & Gedling'; renamed 'Carlton & Netherfield' 1.11.1896; renamed 'Carlton' 6.5.1974; still open for passengers (2010)
Carlton-on-Trent	GNR	1.8.1852 (passengers); 15.7.1852 (goods)	2.3.1953 (passengers); 1.12.1955 (goods)	
Carrington	GCR	15.3.1899	24.9.1928	no facilities for goods
Checker House	MS&LR	1.4.1852 (passenger and goods); 31.10.1960 (goods)	14.9.1931 (passengers); 1.10.1956 (goods); 9.12.1963 (goods)	
Clifton-on-Trent	LD&ECR	15.12.1896	19.9.1955 (passengers); 30.3.1964 (goods)	

Table 3

Collingham	MR	4.8.1846	27.4.1964 (goods)	still open for passengers (2010)
Cotham	GNR	14.4.1879 (passengers); 1.7.1878 (goods); 1.4.1919 (passengers)	2.4.1917 (passengers); 11.9.1939 (passengers); 3.2.1964 (goods)	
Cottam	MS&LR	1850 (passengers); 1889 (goods & cattle)	2.11.1959	temporary station opened at the end of 1850 with permanent building completed early in 1853
Crow Park (for Sutton-on-Trent)	GNR	1.11.1882	6.10.1958 (passengers); 4.5.1964 (goods)	
Daybrook	GNR	1.2.1876	12.3.1962 (passengers); 1.6.1964 (goods)	originally named 'Bestwood & Arnold'; renamed 'Daybrook for Arnold & Bestwood' 1.3.1876
Doddington & Harby	LD&ECR	15.12.1896	19.9.1955 (passengers); 30.3.1964 (goods)	
Dukeries Junction	GNR and LD&ECR	15.12.1896	6.3.1950	no facilities for goods
East Leake	GCR	15.3.1899 (passengers); 11.4.1899 (goods)	5.5.1969 (passengers); 4.3.1968 (goods)	
East Midlands Parkway	NR	26.1.2009		no facilities for goods; still open for passengers (2010)
Eastwood & Langley Mill	GNR	1.8.1876	7.1.1963 (passengers); 2.11.1964 (goods)	
Edwalton	MR	2.2.1880 (passengers); 1.11.1879 (goods)	28.7.1941 (passengers); 1.11.1965 (goods)	
Edwinstowe	LD&ECR	15.12.1896	2.1.1956 (passengers); 4.1.1965 (goods)	passengers continued to use the station to catch summer Saturday only trains to Skegness until 5.9.1964
Elton & Orston	ANBEJR	15.7.1850	30.3.1964 (goods)	still open for passengers (2010)
Farnsfield	MR	3.4.1871	12.8.1929 (passengers); 27.4.1964 (goods)	a replacement bus service was laid on by the LMS when the station closed to passengers
Fiskerton	MR	4.8.1846	15.6.1964 (goods)	still open for passengers (2010)
Fledborough	LD&ECR	15.12.1896	19.9.1955 (passengers); 4.1.1965 (goods)	
Gedling	GNR	1.2.1876	4.4.1960	originally named 'Gedling & Carlton'
Hathern	MR	17.2.1868	1.1.1960 (passengers); 4.1.1960 (goods)	
Hollinwell & Annesley	GCR	1.11.1901	10.9.1962	no facilities for goods
Hucknall	MR	2.10.1848	12.1895 (passengers)	
Hucknall Byron	MR	22.12.1895	12.10.1964 (passengers); 5.5.1952 (goods)	originally named 'Hucknall' until 1.7.1950 (goods) and 11.8.1952 (passengers)
Hucknall	BR	8.5.1993		built on the site of the 1895 MR station; no facilities for goods; still open for passengers (2010)
Hucknall Town	GNR	2.10.1882	14.9.1931 (passengers); 3.5.1965 (goods)	originally named 'Hucknall' until 1.7.1923
Hucknall Central	GCR	15.3.1899 (passengers); 11.4.1899 (goods)	4.4.1963	originally named 'Hucknall Town' until 1.7.1923
Ilkeston Junction & Cossall	MR	6.9.1847	2.1.1967 (passenger & goods)	originally named 'Ilkeston Junction' until 1.12.1890
Jacksdale	GNR	1.8.1876	7.1.1963	originally named 'Codnor Park & Selston'; renamed Codnor Park 22.5.1901; renamed Jacksdale 1.7.1950
Kegworth	MCR	5.5.1840	4.3.1968 (passengers); 5.7.1965 (goods)	
Kimberley	MR	1.9.1882 (passengers); 8.1880 (goods)	1.1.1917 (passengers); 1.1.1951 (goods)	renamed 'Kimberley West' 1.7.1950 when in use only for goods traffic
Kimberley East	GNR	1.8.1876	7.9.1964 (passengers); 2.11.1964 (goods)	originally named 'Kimberley' until the suffix 'East' was added for goods 1.7.1950, and passengers 13.6.1955
Kirklington	MR	3.4.1871	12.8.1929 (passengers); 25.5.1964 (goods)	renamed 'Kirklington & Edingley' 1.9.1871; reverted to 'Kirklington' 1.4.1904; a replacement bus service was laid on by the LMS when the station closed to passengers
Kirkby Bentinck	GCR	2.1.1893 (passengers); 24.10.1892 (goods)	4.3.1963	originally named 'Kirkby & Pinxton' until 1.3.1925
Kirkby-in-Ashfield East	MR	2.10.1848	12.10.1964 (passengers); 6.1.1964 (goods)	originally named 'Kirkby' until renamed 'Kirkby-in-Ashfield' 1.1.1901; suffix 'East' added 1.7.1950 (goods) and 11.8.1952 (passengers)
Kirkby-in-Ashfield Central	GCR (Mansfield Railway)	2.4.1917 (passengers); 4.9.1916 (goods)	2.1.1956	
Kirkby-in-Ashfield	RT	17.11.1996		no facilities for goods; still open for passengers (2010)

Table 3

Lenton	MR	2.10.1848	1.7.1911 (passengers); 4.5.1953 (goods)	
Leverton	MS&LR	1850	2.11.1959	temporary station opened at the end of 1850 with permanent building completed early in 1853
Linby	MR	2.10.1848	12.10.1964 (passengers); 6.1.1964 (goods)	
Linby	GNR	2.10.1882	1.7.1916	
Lowdham	MR	4.8.1846	15.6.1964 (goods)	still open for passengers (2010)
Mansfield	MR	9.10.1849	3.1872 (passengers)	converted for goods use by 1875
Mansfield Central	GCR (Mansfield Railway)	2.4.1917 (passengers); 4.9.1916 (goods)	2.1.1956 (passengers); 13.6.1966 (goods)	originally named 'Mansfield' until 1.7.1950
Mansfield Town	MR	1.3.1872; 20.11.1995	12.10.1964 (passengers); 2.6.1975 (goods)	originally named 'Mansfield' until 1.7.1950 (goods) and 11.8.1952 (passengers); still open for passengers (2010)
Mansfield Woodhouse	MR	1.6.1875 (passengers); 18.1.1875 (goods)	12.10.1964 (passengers); 2.1.1967 (goods)	
Mansfield Woodhouse	RT	20.11.1995		1875 goods warehouse used as temporary terminus until 24.5.1998; no facilities for goods; still open for passengers (2010)
Misterton	GNR	15.7.1867 (passengers); 1.7.1867 (goods)	11.9.1961 (passengers); 6.1.1969 (goods)	
Netherfield	GNR	5.1878?	5.8.1968 (goods)	originally named 'Colwick' until 1.5.1883 when renamed 'Netherfield & Colwick'; renamed 'Netherfield' 8.1901; renamed 'Netherfield & Colwick' 13.7.1925 until 6.5.1974; still open for passengers (2010)
New Basford	GCR	15.3.1899	7.9.1964 (passengers); 2.10.1967 (goods)	
Newark Castle	MR	4.8.1846	4.4.1983 (goods)	originally named 'Newark' until 25.9.1950; still open for passengers (2010)
Newark Northgate	GNR	1.8.1852 (passengers); 15.7.1852 (goods)	4.1985 (goods)	originally named 'Newark" until 25.9.1950; still open for passengers (2010)
Newstead	MR	1.7.1883	12.10.1964 (passengers); 6.1.1964 (goods)	originally opened for private use 4.1863
Newstead	BR	8.5.1993		built close to the site of the original MR station; no facilities for goods; still open for passengers (2010)
Newstead	GNR	2.10.1882	14.9.1931 (passengers); 31.12.1951 (goods)	renamed 'Newstead & Annesley' 7.1891; suffix 'East' added 1.7.1950 when in goods use only
Newthorpe, Greasley & Shipley Gate	GNR	1.8.1876	7.1.1963 (passengers); 2.11.1964 (goods)	station name boards only carried the lettering 'Newthorpe & Greasley'
Nottingham	MCR	4.6.1839	22.5.1848 (passengers)	(situated to the west of Carrington Street); used as goods station until demolished 1873/74
Nottingham	MR	22.5.1848	1.1904 (passengers)	(entrance on Station Street); demolished shortly after closure
Nottingham	MR	17.1.1904		renamed 'Nottingham City' 25.9.1950; renamed 'Nottingham Midland' 18.6.1951; still open for passengers (2010)
Nottingham London Road (Low Level)	ANBEJR	3.10.1857; 1968 (parcels)	12.5.1944 (passengers); 5.9.1966 (livestock); 6.11.1967 (coal); 1.6.1981 (parcels)	originally named 'Nottingham London Road' until 3.1899; complete closure to goods traffic is recorded by C.R. Clinker as 4.12.1972
Nottingham London Road (High Level)	GNR	15.3.1899	3.7.1967	no facilities for goods
Nottingham Race Course	GNR	1892?	9.12.1959	no facilities for goods
Nottingham Victoria	GN&GCJ	24.5.1900	4.9.1967	originally named 'Nottingham Joint Station' by the GNR, and 'Nottingham Central' by the GCR until 12.6.1900
Ollerton	LD&ECR	15.12.1896	19.9.1955 (passengers); 30.12.1968 (goods)	passengers continued to use the station to catch summer Saturday only trains to Skegness until 5.9.1964
Pinxton South (passengers)	GNR	1.8.1876	7.1.1963	suffix 'South' added 1.7.1950 (goods) and 1.1954
Pinxton & Selston	MR	6.11.1851?	16.6.1947 (passengers); 2.11.1964	when being used just for goods, renamed 'Pinxton North' 1.7.1950
Plumtree	MR	2.2.1880 (passengers); 1.11.1879 (goods)	28.2.1949 (passengers); 1.11.1965 (goods)	originally named 'Plumtree & Keyworth' until 5.1893

Table 3

Pye Bridge	MR	1.12.1851	2.1.1967 (passengers); 2.11.1964 (goods)	originally named 'Pye Bridge for Alfreton' until 1.5.1862; station remodelled 1900/1
Pye Hill	GNR	24.3.1877 or 3.4.1877	1899	
Pye Hill & Somercotes	GNR	1899	7.1.1963	located further north than the 1877 station; originally named 'Pye Hill' until 8.1.1906
Radcliffe	ANBEJR	15.7.1850	15.6.1964 (goods)	renamed 'Radcliffe-on-Trent' 1.1.1878; reverted to 'Radcliffe' 6.5.1974; still open for passengers (2010)
Radford	MR	2.10.1848	9.1876	replaced by new station when junction was remodelled (see below)
Radford	MR	10.9.1876	12.10.1964 (passengers); 28.4.1969 (goods)	
Ranskill	GNR	4.9.1849	6.10.1958 (passengers); 7.12.1964 (goods)	
Retford	MS&LR	16.7.1849	1.7.1859	
Retford	GNR	4.9.1849	3.10.1966 (Babworth goods); 7.12.1970 (Thrumpton goods)	platforms provided on the realigned former MS&LR line came into use 14.6.1965; still open for passengers (2010)
Rolleston	MR	1.9.1860		officially named 'Rolleston Junction' 1.11.1860; renamed 'Rolleston' 7.5.1973; still open for passengers (2010)
Ruddington	GCR	15.3.1899 (passengers); 11.4.1899 (goods)	4.3.1963 (passengers); 1.5.1967 (goods)	
Rushcliffe Halt	GCR	3.7.1911	4.3.1963	no facilities for goods
Scrooby	GNR	4.9.1849	14.9.1931	
Sherwood	NSR	2.12.1889	1.7.1931 (passengers); 1.1931 (goods)	
Shireoaks	MS&LR	16.7.1849	9.12.1963 (goods)	still open for passengers (2010)
Skegby	GNR	4.4.1898 (passengers); 1.3.1898 (goods)	14.9.1931 (passengers); 4.8.1952	
Southwell	MR	1.7.1847; 12.4.1852 (passengers); 1.9.1860	1.8.1849; 14.3.1853 (passengers and goods); 15.6.1959 (passengers); 7.12.1964 (goods)	became a through station 3.1871
Southwell Junction	MR	1.7.1847; 12.4.1852	1.8.1849; 14.3.1853	sited at the junction where the Southwell line branched off the Nottingham-Lincoln line (see Rolleston)
St. Ann's Well	NSR	2.12.1889	1.7.1916 (passengers); 1.8.1951 (goods)	
Sandiacre & Stapleford	MR	6.9.1847	5.1872	replaced by new station on same site
Stapleford & Sandiacre	MR	1.5.1872	2.1.1967 (passengers); 5.10.1964 (goods)	originally named 'Sandiacre & Stapleford"
Sturton	MS&LR	16.7.1849	2.2.1959 (passengers); 6.4.1964 (goods)	
Sutton Junction	MR	1849?	12.10.1964 (passengers); 6.1.1964 (goods)	renamed 'Sutton-in-Ashfield' 1.11.1883; renamed 'Sutton Junction' 24.4.1893
Sutton Parkway	RT	20.11.1995		no facilities for goods; still open for passengers (2010)
Sutton-in-Ashfield Town	MR	1.5.1893 (passengers); 20.11.1892 (goods); 9.7.1923 (passengers); 20.9.1926 (passengers and goods)	1.1.1917 (passengers); 4.5.1926 (passenger and goods); 26.9.1949 (passengers); 1.10.1951	originally named 'Sutton-in-Ashfield' until 1.7.1923; renamed 'Sutton-in-Ashfield General' 1.7.1950 when in use only for goods traffic
Sutton-in-Ashfield Town	GNR	4.4.1898 (passengers); 1.3.1898 (goods); 20.2.1956 (passengers)	14.9.1931 (passengers); 17.9.1956 (passengers); 1.2.1965 (goods)	originally named 'Sutton-in-Ashfield' until 1.10.1923
Sutton-in-Ashfield Central	GCR (Mansfield Railway)	2.4.1917 (passengers); 4.9.1916 (goods)	2.1.1956	originally named 'Sutton-in-Ashfield' until 1.7.1923
Teversal	MR	1.5.1886 (passengers); 1.5.1866 (goods)	28.7.1930 (passengers); 7.10.1963	continued to be used for excursions until 7.10.1963; when being used just for goods, renamed 'Teversal Manor' 1.7.1950
Teversal East	GNR	1.3.1898 (goods)	1.10.1951	originally named Teversal until 1.7.1950; the station was used by passenger trains but not as part of a regular, advertised public service
Thorneywood	NSR	2.12.1889	1.7.1931 (passengers); 1.1931 (goods)	
Thurgarton	MR	4.8.1846	7.12.1964 (goods)	still open for passengers (2010)
Trowell	MR	2.6.1884	2.1.1967 (passengers); 2.11.1964 (goods)	

Table 3

Tuxford North	GNR	1.8.1852 (passengers); 15.7.1852 (goods)	4.7.1955 (passengers); 15.6.1964	originally named 'Tuxford' until 1.7.1923
Tuxford Central	LD&ECR	15.12.1896	19.9.1955	originally named 'Tuxford' until 1.7.1923
Upper Broughton	MR	2.2.1880	31.5.1948 (passengers & goods)	
Walkeringham	GNR	15.7.1867 (passengers); 1.7.1867 (goods)	2.2.1959 (passengers); 19.8.1963 (goods)	
Warsop	LD&ECR	8.3.1897	19.9.1955 (passengers); 4.1.1965 (goods)	passengers continued to use the station to catch summer Saturday only trains to Skegness until 5.9.1964
Watnall	MR	1.9.1882	1.1.1917 (passengers); 1.2.1954 (goods)	
Widmerpool	MR	2.2.1880 (passengers); 1.11.1879 (goods)	28.2.1949 (passengers); 1.3.1965 (goods)	
Winthorpe	MR	1.1847?	10.1847?	originally a 'request stop' adjacent to the level crossing on the Winthorpe to Holme road
Worksop	MS&LR	16.7.1849	1980s (goods)?	still open for passengers (2010)

ANBEJR	- Ambergate, Nottingham & Boston & Eastern Junction Railway
BR	- British Rail
GCR	- Great Central Railway
GNR	- Great Northern Railway
GN&GCJ	- Great Northern & Great Central Joint (Nottingham Joint Station Committee)
GN&LNWJR	- Great Northern & London North Western Joint Railway
LD&ECR	- Lancashire, Derbyshire & East Coast Railway
MCR	- Midland Counties Railway
M&GNJR	- Midland & Great Northern Joint Railway
MR	- Midland Railway
MS&LR	- Manchester, Sheffield & Lincolnshire Railway
NR	- Network Rail
NSR	- Nottingham Suburban Railway
RT	- RailTrack

Its apple green livery, brass and steel, polished to a high shine, 4-4-0 no.1316 waits in the GNR's Daybrook station with a couple of carriages for Nottingham Victoria station in September 1912. *(photo: F. Gillford/R.K. Blencowe Negative Archive)*

Index

Index